SOLDIERS of the AMERICAN REVOLUTION

WHO AT ONE TIME WERE RESIDENTS OF, OR WHOSE GRAVES ARE LOCATED IN CHAUTAUQUA COUNTY, NEW YORK

Chautauqua County, New York Chapters
National Society of the
Daughters of the American Revolution

ELLICOTT CHAPTER, D.A.R., FALCONER, N.Y.
BENJAMIN PRESCOTT CHAPTER, D.A.R., FREDONIA, N.Y.
JAMESTOWN CHAPTER, D.A.R., JAMESTOWN, N.Y.
BENJAMIN BOSWORTH CHAPTER, D.A.R., SILVER CREEK, N.Y.
PATTERSON CHAPTER, D.A.R., WESTFIELD, N.Y.

HERITAGE BOOKS
2009

HERITAGE BOOKS
AN IMPRINT OF HERITAGE BOOKS, INC.

Books, CDs, and more—Worldwide

For our listing of thousands of titles see our website
at
www.HeritageBooks.com

A Facsimile Reprint
Published 2009 by
HERITAGE BOOKS, INC.
Publishing Division
100 Railroad Ave. #104
Westminster, Maryland 21157

Originally published 1925
Chautauqua County, New York

— Publisher's Notice —
In reprints such as this, it is often not possible to remove blemishes from the original. We feel the contents of this book warrant its reissue despite these blemishes and hope you will agree and read it with pleasure.

International Standard Book Numbers
Paperbound: 978-0-7884-2082-5
Clothbound: 978-0-7884-8059-1

PREFACE

IT has required much earnest effort and careful research to obtain and arrange the brief account of the services, personal and military, of the valiant Soldiers of the American Revolution, who, at one time resided in, or whose graves are located in Chautauqua County, N. Y.

The Historical Committees of the several Chapters of the Daughters of American Revolution, located in Chautauqua County, have been most painstaking as well as zealous in their work, and what is written in this little booklet is believed to be quite as authentic and correct as it has been possible to obtain from the records that have been found. The records, both military and personal, have been mainly supplied from official pension papers as well as from family records, local history, and the files of early local newspapers.

It has been a work of real pleasure to the members of the local Committees to assist in paying a most deserved and merited tribute to the memory of those self-sacrificing, patriotic, great soldiers who achieved so much and gave us the heritage of the Country's independence and freedom.

The Soldiers of the American Revolution remain in a distinct class of the world's history—with only the poorest and most meagre equipment, they eagerly responded to the first call of Lexington and Bunker Hill, facing every danger with unsurpassed courage, willingly sacrificing every personal comfort, suffering and enduring beyond description, but with sturdy hearts and conscience unyielding to the end that freedom and liberty might be their country's right for all time.

Just a look back to Valley Forge in the winter of 1778, described by the historian, Headley, is a revelation of what the Soldiers of the American Revolution suffered, braved, and the wonderful record of their heroic character:

"Eleven thousand American Soldiers, two thousand of whom were barefoot and half naked, stacked their arms in the latter part of December, in the frozen field, and began to look for huts to shelter them from the cold of winter. Hundreds with nothing but rags upon their bodies, their muskets resting upon their naked shoulders, their bare feet cut by the frozen ground till you could track them by their blood, had marched hither for repose and clothing, and, alas, nothing but the frost-covered fields received them. Starving, wretched and wan, they looked like the wreck of a routed and famine struck army. Without a mouthful of meat to satisfy their hunger they thus passsed days and weeks, and yet not a movement of dissension."

An even measure of praise may be accorded the bravery, fortitude and unyielding spirit of the women soldiers of the American Revolution, the wives and mothers, fully as heroic as those who directly faced the enemy, with a buoyant hope and unfaltering courage unsurpassed in history.

No pen can do full justice to the great character of those pioneer settlers of Chautauqua County, who, with their comrades, gave the world such a wonderful demonstration of success in their great fight for the inherent rights of mankind in the pursuit of peace, happiness, progress and their country's road to greatness.

LUCY NORTON SHANKLAND,
Chairman Research Committee.

Spirit of '76

Stirred to action by fife and drum the Soldiers of '76 fought the great fight for American Independence and the equality of human rights.

Chapter List of Soldiers

List of Ellicott Chapter, D. A. R., Falconer, N. Y.

Allen, Phineas
Baker, Seth
Bill, Jonathan
Davis, Paul
Fenton, Nathaniel
Hamlin, Cyrenus
Hitchcock, Abijah

Mather, Stephen
Mathews, Benjamin
Reynolds, Joel
Tracey, Elias
Woodward, John
Woodward, Joshua

List of Benjamin Prescott Chapter, D. A. R., Fredonia, N.Y.

Atkins, Amos
Abel, Thomas
Barker, Hezekiah
Barnes, Daniel
Batcheler, Abraham
Bovee, Nicholas
Brigham, John
Burnham, Augustus
Carter, Elias
Carter, Elijah
Clark, Caleb
Cleland, John
Cole, Seth
Coney, John
Crosby, Simon
Curtice, Thomas
Deming, Daniel
Dunn, Capt. James
Fitch, Roswell
Fox, Veniah
Gates, Luther
Gleason, Jacob
Goldsmith, James
Gugle, Joseph
Hempstead, Nathaniel
Hill, Zimri
Hood, William
Johnson, Nathaniel
Kane, Peter

Lamont, William
Light, John
Lowell, Willoughby
Marsh, Silas
Moore, King
Munson, Samuel
Parker, Samuel
Peters, Joseph Phelps
Phelps, Jonathan
Potter, Capt. Jeremiah
Risley, Elijah
Rood, Jeremiah
Rood, Joseph
Seaver, Robert W.
Seymour, William
Shattuck, Samuel
Sinclair, Samuel
Smith, Ebenezer
Smith, Israel
Stone, Isaac
Taylor, Reuben
Thompson, Reuben
Tucker, Capt. Samuel
Turner, Asa
Walker, Lewis
Webster, Elisha
Wiard, Darius
Wood, Nathan

CHAPTER LISTS OF SOLDIERS

List of Jamestown Chapter, D. A. R., Jamestown, N. Y.

Adams, William
Annis, Jacob
Babcock, Jonathan
Bacon, Lemuel
Barney, Luther
Beebee, Amon
Bemus, William
Benedict, Samuel
Boyd, Joseph
Campbell, John
Chamberlain, Phineas
Cheney, Ebenezer
Cleveland, Gardiner
Coe, John
Comstock, Martin L.
Covel, Benjamin
Cowing, John
Crawford, Andrew
Davis, Samuel
Delamater, Benjamin
Dix, Joseph
Ely, William
Fenton, Adonijah
Fenton, Jacob
Fish, Cyrus
Frank, Lawrence
Griffith, Jeremiah
Hazeltine, Daniel
Hollister, David
Ives, Enos
Jones, John
Landon, Reuben
Look, Elijah
Loomis, Simon
Loucks, Joseph

Maples, Josiah
Marsh, Jasper
Martin, Aaron
Martin, William
Mather, Nathaniel
Mathews, Thomas
Matteson, William
Moore, Asa
Owen, John
Osborn, Isaac
Palmiter, Phineas
Parker, Benjamin
Pickard, John
Pier, Levi
Rhodes, John
Scofield, Seely
Scofield, William
Smiley, John B.
Smiley, William
Staples, Isaac
Stearns, Capt. William
Stedman, Levi
Steward, Eliphalet
Stow, John
Washburn, William
Waterbury, Samuel
Wellman, Barnabus
Wellman, John
Whitney, Richard
Wilcox, Stephen
Williams, Daniel
Wing, Daniel
Wood, Charles
Young, Samuel

List of Benjamin Bosworth Chapter, D. A. R., Silver Creek, N. Y.

Allen, Moses
Ball, Mathias
Barnes, Reuben
Bush, Stephen
Clark, Elias

Cooley, Abner
Cranston, Samuel
Clothier, Jesse
Darling, John
Ensign, Otis

CHAPTER LISTS OF SOLDIERS

List of Benjamin Bosworth Chapter, D.A.R., Silver Creek, N. Y. (Continued)

Ferry, John
Ferry, Susannah
Frink, Thomas
Gage, Asa
Gregory, Esbon
Hatch, Nathan
Holmes, Orsamus
Herrick, Ephriam
Ingraham, Amos
Ingraham, William
Hamlin, Zacchias
Johnson, John
Kent, John
Kirkland, William
Love, Robert
Mather, Joseph
McManus, Christopher
Nash, Silas
Naughton, Solomon
Nevins, Thomas
Olmstead, James
Osborne, Daniel
Phelps, Cornelius
Phillips, Thomas
Pratt, Stephen
Rathbun, Solomon
Schofield, Enos
Spencer, Reuben
Spencer, John
Spink, Shibnah
Thatcher, Eliakim
Thompson, Nathan
Van Camp, Isaac
Warner, Nathaniel
White, James
Wood, William

List of Patterson Chapter, D. A. R., Westfield, N. Y.

Adams, Levi
Anderson, Samuel
Barns, Calvin
Barnhart, Peter
Burnham, Daniel
Bell, Arthur
Bennett, Benjamin
Benson, Joel
Bird, Nathaniel
Bond, Bethuel
Bradley, Lent
Brigham, Jonathan
Chase, William
Couch, William
Darrow, George
Dickson, Robert
Dustin, Moses
Durand, Fisk
Dyer, Jonathan
Findley, Alexander
Hale, Josiah
Hall, John
Houghton, Silas
House, John
Madden, David
McGregor, Capt. David
Morse, Josiah
Nichols, Jonathan
Penfield, Samuel
Rice, Peletiah
Rumsey, David
Selden, Benjamin
Spencer, Orange
Standish, Amos
Stetson, Oliver
Tennant, Daniel
Thayer, Joseph
Turner, William
Waldo, David
Winters, Juvenile
Wheeler, Samuel
Wright, Reuben
Wells, Asa

Ellicott Chapter, D. A. R.
Falconer, N. Y.

Regent: ELIZABETH NEEDLE DAILY
Historical Committee: MYRTLE B. REED
ELIZABETH NEEDLE DAILY
ADELE HOOKER JOHNSON

Soldiers of the American Revolution who at one time resided in, or whose graves are located in one of the towns of Carroll, Ellington, Gerry, Poland, Chautauqua County, N. Y.

ALLEN, PHINEAS—Born 1758. Died Sept. 6, 1851, aged 93 years. Grave in Allen Cemetery, town of Poland. It is believed that he came to Chautauqua County with his son, Sumner Allen, who settled in the town of Poland in 1818. He enlisted in the American army at Groton, Conn., May or June, 1777. Served three years as private in Connecticut Militia under Capt. John Shumway and Cols. Huntington, Prentiss and Starr. Was at battle of Monmouth. His wife, Sibbil, died Dec. 21, 1846, aged 80 years, and is buried beside him in Allen Cemetery. He is mentioned in Pension List of 1840. Their son, Sumner Allen, born in 1804 in Otsego Co., N. Y., settled in the town of Poland in 1818, and during his life was prominent in the affairs of the town. His wife was Fluvia, daughter of Col. Nathaniel Fenton. They left many descendants.

BAKER, SETH—Born May 5, 1762. in Dighton, Mass. Died June 5, 1842, aged 80 years. Grave in Levant Cemetery, town of Poland. Enlisted in the American army April or May 7, 1777, at Dighton, Mass. Served as marine under Capt. Rathbone, on sloop "Providence" in Massachusetts; also served under Capt. Olney and Col. Crary in Rhode Island militia, and as teamster under Wagonmaster Shields in Mass. His name appears on the Pension List of 1840 as residing in the town of Poland, Chautauqua County, N. Y. Was married in 1787 in Mass. His wife, Cynthia Briggs, died May 5, 1837, aged 68 years. Her grave is beside her husband in the Levant Cemetery.

BILL, JONATHAN—Born April 21, 1756. Died January 19, 1843, aged 88 years. Grave in Dry Brook Cemetery, town of Poland. At the commencement of the Revolution he joined the Continental army and served seven years. He was at the Battle of Bunker Hill, marched in the army of Benedict Arnold to Quebec and was at the storming of that city. He also participated in the engagements at Trenton, Monmouth and Valley Forge. He and his wife, Acenath, were natives of Massachusetts. With his sons, Joseph and Norton Bill, he emigrated to Chautauqua County in 1832 and settled in the town of Poland. He is mentioned as a pensioner in the Census of 1840 and residing with his son Joseph Bill in the town of Poland.

DAVIS, PAUL—Born at Medford, Mass., Nov. 10, 1760. Died at Kiantone, Chautauqua County, N. Y., December 28, 1826, aged 66 years, 1 month and 18 days. Grave in Falconer Cemetery, town of Ellicott. He enlisted as a private in the Continental army in the year 1778, at the age of 18 years, served as Sergeant in

Capt. Abner Dow's Company, Col. Bigelow's Reg't, Massachusetts Militia. He was at West Point in 1781 under Capt. Phineas Bowman and Col. Rufus Putnam. Near the close of the war he served in the Company of Captain Sylvanus Smith and received an honorable discharge at its close. His father was Moses Davis and his mother was Priscilla Wood. He was united in marriage with Rachel Chapin in 1783, whose death occurred June 28, 1823, aged 59 years, 1 month and 21 days. Her grave is beside her husband in Falconer Cemetery. He followed his boyhood friends of Meridon, Mass., Asey Moore and Eben Cheney, to Chautauqua County in 1815. He became a Baptist minister and was locally known as a gifted singer.

FENTON, NATHANIEL—Born March 26, 1763, at Mansfield, Conn. Died January 25, 1846, aged 83 years. Grave in Allen Cemetery, town of Poland. Enlisted in American army at Mansfield, Conn., in August 1779 under Col. Abbott, and from May, 1780, to Dec., 1780, under Col. Stare, and from April, 1781, for one year under Col. Dana. He was awarded a pension and is mentioned in the Pension List of 1840. After the war he resided for a time at Mansfield, Conn. In 1791 he moved to Otsego County, N. Y., and in Sept., 1823, moved to Chautauqua County, locating on lot 58 in the town of Poland. He served as a member of the Board of Supervisors from the town of Ellicott in 1827-28 and from the town of Poland in 1832. He was prominent and an active citizen and was locally known as Colonel Fenton. His last public act was the reading of the Declaration of Independence on the 4th of July, 1843. His wife was Rachel Fletcher, who was born in 1766, and whose death occurred Sept. 1, 1842. Her grave is beside husband. They had five children: Orrilla, Fanny, Elsie, Richard F., and Fluvia. He was a brother of Jacob Fenton, Revolutionary soldier, who settled in Chautauqua County in 1812.

HAMLIN, CYRENUS—Born 1753. Died at Kennedy, Chautauqua County, October 3, 1843. Grave in Riverside Cemetery, Kennedy, town of Poland. One of his ancestors, James Hamlin, came from London, England, in 1639, and settled in Massachusetts. Cyrenus served 7 years in American army. He moved from Charlton, Saratoga County, N. Y., to Chautauqua County in 1833. He had seven children, Perez, Mercy, Laura, Clarissa, Elizabeth, Seth, Milo. It is of record that the last years of his life were spent at the home of his daughter Elizabeth Merritt, in the town of Poland and that he was afflicted with blindness.

HITCHCOCK, ABIJAH—Born May 14, 1759. Died April 9, 1844, aged 84 years, 10 months and 25 days. Grave in Ellington Cemetery, town of Ellington. Enlisted May, 1777, at Brimfield, Mass. Served three years as private under Captain Toogood and Col. Nixon in Mass. Militia. Was at the battle of Saratoga, at the taking of Burgoyne. Is mentioned in the Pension List of 1840. Was united in marriage to Miriam Gilbert, Dec. 3, 1782. Was married to Anna Bliss, August 3, 1795. She was born Dec. 9, 1773, in Wilbreham, Mass. Her death occurred Dec. 6, 1863, aged 90 years. A daughter was born in 1799. A daughter Anna, son Onerimus and two other children were born to them. They moved to New York state at an early date.

MATHER, STEPHEN—Born at Lyme, Conn., Feb. 9, 1758. Died June 7, 1837, aged 79 years. Grave in Clear Creek Cemetery, town of Ellington. His wife, Elizabeth Peck, born at Lyme, Conn., Jan. 5th, 1760, died April 12th,

1839, aged 79 years. Grave beside husband. They were married in 1781. Was Revolutionary soldier and brother of Joseph Mather, also Revolutionary soldier.

MATHEWS, BENJAMIN—Born 1755 in Rhode Island. Died January 13, 1843, aged 88 years, 7 months and 2 days. Grave in Gerry Hill Cemetery, town of Gerry. Enlisted May 7, 1775, at Providence, R. I., served as private under Capt. Thayer and Col. Hitchcock. Re-enlisted Jan. 1st, 1776, served one year. Re-enlisted in June 1778, served 9 months. Was at the battle of Harlem Heights. He is mentioned in the Pension List of 1840 as residing in the town of Gerry, aged 85 years and residing with Caleb Mathews.

REYNOLDS, JOEL—Born October 16, 1760, at Charlotte, Dutchess County, N. Y. He is mentioned in the Pension List of 1840, as 79 years of age and residing with Joel J. Reynolds, in the town of Poland, Chautauqua County, N. Y. He enlisted Aug. 1st, 1777 to Oct. 31, 1777, serving under Capt. James Talmadge and Col. Graham. Enlisted Nov. 1st, 1777, served six months under Capt. Bell. Enlisted again in Aug. 1779 and in June 1780. His residence at time of enlistment, Charlotte, N. Y. The location of his grave not known. Was granted a pension in 1833 while residing in the town of Poland.

TRACEY, ELIAS—Born April 6, 1763. Died May 24, 1848, aged 85 years, 1 month and 18 days. Grave in Allen Cemetery, town of Poland. Enlisted at Preston, Conn., in American army. Re-enlisted April, 1778, serving in Capt. Wheeler's Company, Col. Chapman's Reg't, Vermont troops. His total service in army was between 3 and 4 years. Was granted pension in 1833 and is mentioned in the Pension List of 1840 as residing in the town of Poland, Chautauqua County. His wife, Lydia Gates, died April 25th, 1845, aged 79 years, and is buried beside husband in Allen Cemetery. It is said he was a very religious and somewhat eccentric man and when he emigrated with his family from Chelsea, Vermont, to Chautauqua County, in 1816, he brought with him a horse and some sheep, butchering the latter for food along the overland trip. He was one of the original purchasers of land in the town of Poland.

WOODWARD, JOHN—Born August 7, 1757, at Plainfield, Conn. Died June 12, 1845, aged 88 years. Grave in Riverside Cemetery, Kennedy, town of Poland. He enlisted in January, 1776, and served 4 months; again enlisted in Capt. Bannister's Company of Col. Moseley's Reg't. Sept., 1776, and served 6 months; re-enlisted in Capt. Cook's Company, of Col. Sprout's Reg't and served nine months, and again in same Regiment in 1781, serving eight months. He was married to Sally Galloway in Conway, Mass., March 5, 1786. She died Feb. 21, 1832, at Ellington, N. Y. Her grave is beside her husband in Riverside Cemetery, Kennedy.

WOODWARD, JOSHUA—Born April 11, 1755, at Preston, Windham County, Conn. Died July 10, 1844, aged 89 years, 2 months and 29 days. Grave in Allen Cemetery, town of Poland. In 1775 served nine months in Connecticut Militia under Capt. Avery and Col. Coit. Was at the battle of White Plains and was at attack on Groton Front and burning of New London. In 1787 was married to Experience Jerald. They had a family of eight children. She died March 18, 1822, aged 57 years, and her grave is beside her husband in Allen Cemetery. He is mentioned in the Pension List of 1840 as aged 84 and living with Peer Woodward in the town of Poland. Their children were: Reuben, Sabrina, Sukey, Royal, Lewis, Polly, Pierce, Hiram.

Benjamin Prescott Chapter, D. A. R.
Fredonia, N. Y.

Regent: GRACE HAMILTON GARDINER
Historical Committee: MARIAN F. COOPER
MATTIE RIDER
ELLA I. DAVIS
KATHERINE TARBOX
HARRIET PIER

Soldiers of the American Revolution who at one time resided in, or whose graves are located in one of the towns of Charlotte, Cherry Creek, Dunkirk, Pomfret, Portland, Stockton, Chautauqua County, N. Y.

ATKINS, AMOS — Inscription on grave stone says he was a Revolutionary Soldier. Grave in Pickett Cemetery, town of Charlotte. No record obtained of his military service. He came to Chautauqua Lake about 1808, locating near Wm. Bemus in Ellery, and in 1810 settled in the town of Gerry, built a log house, and in 1814 was chosen supervisor of the town. His wife, Clarinda, died in 1815. This was the first death to occur in the town of Gerry.

ABEL, THOMAS—Born Oct. 9, 1749 at Norwich, Conn. Died Oct. 10, 1814 at Fredonia. Grave in Fredonia Cemetery. He married Eunice Griswold who was born at Norwich, Conn., Sept. 25, 1752. He served as a private at the Battle of Bennington in 1777, was Sergeant in Col. Samuel Herrick's Reg't of Vermont on October 11, 1780, and ten days thereafter; and responded to an alarm in August, 1781, serving in Col. Herrick's Reg't until September, 1782. He came to Fredonia with his son, Thomas W. Abel about 1815. He left many descendants who were prominent in business circles of Western New York.

BARKER, HEZEKIAH—Born at Newport, R. I., April 14, 1757. Died at Fredonia, N. Y., July 5, 1834. Grave in Cemetery at Fredonia, N. Y. He enlisted at Little Compton, R. I., and served ten months in American army, after which he followed the army of Washington, serving as the dispatch carrier, passing through the enemy lines when necessary and doing great service. Was awarded a pension. He married Sarah Wood at Little Compton, R. I., Nov. 27, 1783. Pension allowed wife after his death. She died Jan. 28, 1851, aged 86 years.

BATCHELLER, ABRAHAM—Born at Sutton, Mass., March 26, 1752. Died at Stockton, Chautauqua County, N. Y., Aug. 14, 1832. Grave in Stockton Cemetery. Enlisted as Corporal under Capt. Andrew Elliot, Col. Ebenezer Learned. Also served under Capt. Reuben Sibley, Col. Jacob Davis. Discharged Aug. 8, 1780. Attained rank of Lieut. Married Rebecca Dwight Dec. 28, 1774.

BARNES, DANIEL—Born at Waterboro, Conn., Dec. 4, 1762. Died in the year 1854 at Portland, Chautauqua County, N. Y. Grave in Portland Cemetery. Enlisted in 1780 at Plymouth, Conn., served in Regiment of Col. Porter. Second enlistment under Capt. Mans-

DAUGHTERS of the AMERICAN REVOLUTION

field and Col. Porter. Third enlistment under Capt. Asahel Hodge, Col. Isaac Sherman, 1782. Was granted pension and mentioned in Pension List of 1840. Married Lucinda King in 1783. She died in 1854. He moved to Portland in 1810. One child Fanny.

BRIGHAM, JOHN—Born 1758. Died at Fredonia Aug. 21, 1828. Grave in Fredonia Cemetery. No record of his family or military service has yet been obtainable, although during his life he was known as a Revolutionary soldier. He was a brother of Jonathan Brigham, Revolutionary soldier, who was a resident of Mayville. John Brigham became a resident of Chautauqua County at an early part of the 19th century, locating in the town of Pomfret. His father, Joel Brigham, was also a Revolutionary soldier.

BOVEE, NICHOLAS—Born about 1759. Date of death and location of grave not ascertained. Served as private in the New York state troops in the war of the Revolution. Was granted a pension in 1831 while residing in Chautauqua County, N. Y., and in the Pension List of 1840 is mentioned as residing with Ebenezer Baldwin in the town of Pomfret.

BURNHAM, AUGUSTUS—Born at Hartford, Conn., Aug. 4, 1751. Died at Laona, Chautauqua County, N. Y., in 1823. Grave in Laona Cemetery. He was united in marriage with Mary Stedman in 1771. She was born in 1753 and died in 1832. He enlisted in Connecticut and marched with the first troops for the relief of Boston at the Lexington Alarm.

CARTER, ELIAS—Born Nov. 24, 1737. Grave in Charlotte Cemetery, town of Charlotte. Enlisted in American army at Leominister, Mass., in 1776, with his son. Little is known of his history. Was married Jan. 12, 1761, at Lunenburg, Mass., to Deborah White, who was born Dec. 24, 1739.

CARTER, ELIJAH—Born at Leominister, Mass., Jan. 16, 1762. Died at Charlotte, Chautauqua County, N. Y., in 1833. Grave in Charlotte Cemetery. He enlisted at the age of 14 years in Massachusetts troops, going with his father, Elias Carter, in 1776. He drew a pension.

CLARK, CALEB—Born about 1758. Died May 17, 1837, aged 79. Grave in Picket Cemetery, town of Charlotte. He enlisted in 2nd New Hampshire Reg't and served in the army four years and two months. He participated in the battles of Trenton, Stillwater and other engagements in New Jersey.

CLELAND, JOHN—Born in 1758. Died at Charlotte, Chautauqua County, N. Y., February 16, 1827. Grave in Pickett Cemetery, town of Charlotte. He enlisted Feb., 1778, in Col. Williss' Reg't, Conn. troops, serving two and one half years. His wife, Thankful Eaton, survived him, and was allowed a pension. In March, 1811, accompanied by their sons, Nathan and Oliver, Mr. and Mrs. Cleland settled in the town of Charlotte where another son, John, Jr., had settled the previous year.

COLE, SETH—Born at Chesterfield, Mass., in 1756. Died in Dunkirk, N. Y., previous to 1812. Grave in Fredonia. Enlisted May 8, 1777, and in Sept., 1777. Again enlisted for nine months and again for nine months. Served as private under Capt. Christopher Bannister and under Capt. Benj. Barney, Col. Ezra May's Reg't; third enlistment under Capt. Weber, Col. Chapin's Reg't. His wife was Celia Sanford and they settled in Dunkirk in 1805. Their daughter, Maria, married David Dodge.

CONEY, JOHN—Born at Boston, Mass., in the year 1753. Died at Portland, Chautauqua County, N. Y., in 1838. Grave in Portland Cemetery. He served two years in the Continental army and Government employ until the close of the war. His father's name was William and his mother's, Betsey Lowell. They came from England. He married Lovina Paterson, at Palmer, Mass., and resided at South Hadley, Mass., until 1807, then removing to Bennington, Vt., and to Portland, N. Y., in 1823. His wife died in Portland in 1852. They left eight children: John, William, Solomon, Oliver, Lowell, Martin, Lucy, Louisa.

CROSBY, SIMON—Born at Brewster, Mass., in 1764. Died at Fredonia, N. Y., Jan. 25, 1837. Grave in Fredonia Cemetery. Enlisted Sept. 29, 1777, served as private under Capt. John Maynard, Col. Job Cushing's Reg't. Served as private in Connecticut troops and was honorably discharged in 1783. He married Hulda Gibbs. A son, Oris Crosby, born, 1790, died 1863.

CURTICE, THOMAS—Born Feb. 6, 1761, at Westerly, R. I. Died April 16, 1843, at Stockton, Chautauqua County, N. Y. Grave in Stockton Cemetery. Enlisted at Stephentown, Rensselaer County, N. Y., April 1779, served nine months under Capt. Isaac Bogart, Col. Henry Van Rensselaer, New York Militia. Second enlistment in 1781 for four months under Capt. Livingston, Col. Van Rensselaer. Battles engaged in: West Canada Creek. His wife was Thankful Crandal. He was granted a pension in 1832 and is mentioned in the Pension List of 1840 as residing with Jeremiah Curtice, at Stockton, Chautauqua County, N. Y.

DEMING, DANIEL—Born at Worthing, Conn., March 28, 1762. Died at Stockton, Chautauqua County, N. Y., Oct. 30, 1848. Grave in Stockton Cemetery. Enlisted at Sanderfield, Mass., 1778, served as private under Sergeant French, marched through Great Barrington, Canaan, Schodack, to Albany. Second enlistment was in May, 1779, at New Lebanon, Columbia County, N. Y., served under Capt. Nobles and Lieut. Lemuel Rexford, marched through Albany to Schoharie and held garrison there under Col. Vrooman. Later was placed under Capt. Cody and dispatched to Fishkill where he served under Col. Waterman until Dec. 1, 1779. Third enlistment June, 1780, served under Capt. Gilbert and Lieut. Rexford at Stillwater and other places. He married Sally Johnson at Kensington, Conn. On 1840 Pension List.

DUNN, Capt. JAMES—Born in Lycoming County, Pa., in 1761. Died at Portland, Chautauqua County, N. Y., Oct. 23, 1838. Family records say he was a Revolutionary soldier. He married Miss Alexander at Mifflin, Pa., in 1791. She was born in South Carolina in 1771. Her death occurred Oct. 23, 1850. James Dunn was the first settler of the town of Portland, purchasing eleven hundred acres of land from the Holland Land Company in 1804 and the next year taking up his residence there in a hut or shanty in which he lived until he could build a more commodious log house in 1806. The first tavern in the settlement was opened by him in 1808. Their children were: William, Eliza, James, Davis, Rebecca, David, John, George, Polly, Jane. George was the first white child born in the town.

FITCH, ROSWELL—Born Dec. 7, 1765. Died in Pomfret, Chautauqua

County, in 1842. Grave in Fredonia Cemetery. Enlisted in the Revolutionary army Dec. 17, 1782, serving under Capt. Josiah Bissell, Col. Levi, Connecticut troops. He was taken prisoner at Horse Neck and confined until 1783. He is mentioned in the Pension List of 1840.

FOX, VENIAH—Born at New Hartford, Conn., 1763. Died at Pomfret, Chautauqua County, N. Y., Feb. 2, 1851. Grave in Fredonia Cemetery. Enlisted at East Hartford, Conn., with Connecticut troops and was at the battle of Rhode Island, West Chester County, Springfield, N. J., Jamestown, Va., and was present at the surrender of Cornwallis at Yorktown. He married Sarah Cadwell March 23, 1784. She was born 1764 and died June 21, 1840. He is mentioned in the Pension List of 1840.

GATES, LUTHER—Born in Preston, Conn., 1761. Died at Pomfret, Chautauqua County, N. Y., Sept. 1826. Grave in Fredonia Cemetery. Enlisted at Windham, Conn., as drummer under Capt. Abner Bacon, Col. John Durkee, serving three years. Second enlistment in 4th Connecticut Reg't, serving until the end of the war. Was at Peekskill, later with Washington's Army in Pennsylvania, was at the battle of Germantown, wintered at Valley Forge and participated in the battle of Monmouth. Was granted a pension. He married Anna Brown at Stephenstown, N. Y., Jan. 1, 1789. She died in 1846.

GLEASON, JACOB—Born at Thompson, Windham County, Conn., July 23, 1768. Died at Stockton, Chautauqua County, N. Y., Oct. 12, 1842. Enlisted with Connecticut troops in 1782, serving two years. He married Rachel Barnes, March 3, 1792, and after her death he was united in marriage with Mehitable Hudson, Jan. 16, 1796. His grave is in Sinclairville Cemetery.

GOLDSMITH, JAMES—Born in Connecticut in 1759. Died in Portland, Chautauqua County, N. Y., Feb. 20, 1837. Grave in Portland Cemetery. Enlisted from Connecticut Feb. 14, 1777, as Sergeant under Capt. Chas. Pond, Col. Return Meigs. Second enlistment under Capt. Asa Lay, Col. Heman Swift. Third enlistment in 1780 under Capt. Phelps, serving until June, 1783. Moved to Portland, Chautauqua County, N. Y., in 1830. His children were: Roe, James, John, Martin, Frederick.

GUGLE, JOSEPH—Born in Connecticut. Died at Portland, Chautauqua County, N. Y., in 1825. Grave in Portland Cemetery. Enlisted with Connecticut troops as private under Captain Barton. He was for some time stationed in Rhode Island and later was in the hazardous adventure under Captain Barton which resulted in the capture of the British General Prescott. His wife was Sally Hunt. Came to Portland in 1815. Children: Simeon, Henry.

HEMPSTEAD, NATHANIEL—Born in Connecticut in 1748. Died at Fredonia, Chautauqua County, N. Y., January 23, 1841. Grave in Fredonia Cemetery. On his tombstone it says he was a Revolutionary soldier, but no further record of his service has been obtained. He became a resident of the town of Pomfret in 1822.

HILL, ZIMRI—Born in Connecticut in 1762. Died at Portland, Chautauqua County, N. Y., Nov. 15, 1843. Grave in Portland Cemetery. No authentic record of his military service has been obtained although his tombstone is marked, "Was a Revolutionary Soldier". Married second wife, Malinda Palmer of Ferrisburg, Vt. Came to Portland in October, 1815.

HOOD, WILLIAM—Born at Providence, R. I., 1762. Died at Pomfret, Chautauqua County, N. Y., August 8, 1858. Grave in Fredonia Cemetery, Pomfret. Enlisted at Vellster County, R. I., as private under Capt. John A. Hardenburg, Col. Levi Pauling's Reg't, Rhode Island Militia. Was granted a pension. He was married three times. His last wife was Sally McLean, born in 1792 and died 1851. Mrs. Elizabeth Hood Perkins was their daughter.

JOHNSON, NATHANIEL—Born in 1763. Died at Jamestown, N. Y., Oct. 31, 1826, while on a visit to his son, Forbes Johnson. Grave in Sinclairville Cemetery. He enlisted in Portsmouth, N. H., Nov. 23, 1777, was mustered into service as private by Joseph Cilley, Mustering Master, in the company of Capt. Henry Elkins, was at the battle of Saratoga and witnessed the surrender of Burgoyne. He married Mary Nye, daughter of Jonathan Nye, who was also a soldier of the Revolution. He emigrated to Western New York in 1813, coming through Buffalo while the ruins were smoking after the town was burned, settled for a time at Hamburg, Silver Creek, then Westfield and finally to Sinclairville where his friend and companion, Samuel Sinclair, who served in the same New Hampshire Reg't, had located. His wife, Mary, died Dec. 11, 1838, aged 74 years. Their daughter, Hannah, married Sylvanus L. Henderson, in 1816, and their son, William W. Henderson, born in 1828, was for many years prominent in the affairs of Chautauqua County. His death occurred in 1910.

KANE, PETER—Date of birth not ascertained. Died January 7th, 1818.

Grave in Evergreen Cemetery, town of Portland, Chautauqua County, N. Y. According to the "Historical Sketches of the Town of Portland," by Dr. Taylor, he was a Revolutionary soldier and also participated in the war of 1812. Came to Portland in 1804 from some place in the Mohawk Valley, settled on part of lot 30, Portland township, and kept a tavern for two years. He was a justice of the peace in 1805 and in 1806 purchased of James Dunn a farm upon which he built a log house where he resided until his death in 1818. After his death his wife went to live with her daughter, Clara, in Erie, Pa., where she died a few years later. Their children were: Polly, Clara, Phillip, Ann.

LAMONT, WILLIAM—Born at Hillsdale, N. Y., in 1756. Died in the town of Pomfret, Chautauqua County, N. Y., Nov. 1, 1848. Enlisted in Oct. 1775, for 3 months in Company of Capt. Joshua Whitney. Enlisted in June, 1778, serving in Company of Capt. Jonas Graves and Capt. Joshua Whitney. In Nov., 1778, and in Aug. and Oct. 1780, served in Company of Capt. Whitney, was at battle of Fort Plain, where Indians and Tories under Sir John Johnson were defeated. May 17, 1800, at Hillsdale, N. Y., he was united in marriage with Mary Rodmond. They had five children and the last years of their lives they spent at the home of their son, Albertus Lamont, in the town of Pomfret, Chautauqua County, N. Y.

LIGHT, JOHN—Born about 1749. Died Oct. 21, 1828, in Westfield, Chautauqua County, N. Y. Grave in Portland Cemetery. Served as private in New York troops in the Revolutionary army, and is mentioned on the Pension List of 1819 as residing in Chautauqua County, N. Y. Little is known of his family his-

17

tory. Came to Portland in 1818. Children: Abigail, Jacob, John, William, Elizabeth, Israel.

LOWELL, WILLOUGHBY—Born at Amesbury, Mass., in May, 1749. Died June 17, 1823. Grave said to be in Portland Cemetery, Portland, Chautauqua County, N. Y. Enlisted May 9, 1775, served in Continental Reg't, 3rd Co., Mass., under Corp. Roger Enos. Married Sally Salvan. She died at Lamberton in 1837 and is buried beside husband in Portland Cemetery. His father's name was Moses Lowell.

MARSH, SILAS—Born May 26, 1764. Died February 25, 1851. Location of grave not ascertained. Was residing in the town of Pomfret in 1840 as his name appears on the Pension List. Enlisted at Lebanon, Conn., in 1782, served as teamster under Capt. Robert Patrick and was engaged in collecting stores, provisions, lumber, etc., for the use of General Washington's army at Verplanck's Point. He was united in marriage Jan. 18, 1787, to Mary Hare. Their children were: Polly, married James Frost; Charles, married Polly Eddy; Silas, married Philomela Burr; Phebe, married Stephen Titus; William, drowned in 1818; Lucy, married Britan Tallman; Ira, married Catharine Gage; Betsey, married James E. O'Neil; Daniel, married Catherine Crookshank; Marcius, died 1826; Louisa, married John C. Wright. In 1855 the widow of Silas Marsh, then 82 years of age, was granted a pension of Bounty Land.

MOORE, KING—Born in Massachusetts in 1762. Died at Pomfret, Chautauqua County, N. Y., April 15, 1857. Grave in Fredonia Cemetery. Enlisted Nov. 1, 1779, under Sergeant White, Capt. Burbank in Col. John Crane's Reg't. Discharged Dec. 31, 1780. Second enlistment, Jan. 11, 1781. Was united in marriage with Rebecca Mitchell, Oct. 19, 1783, at West Springfield, Mass. She died before 1815. Was later married to Susan Tarbox, no record of date of marriage nor death of wife. He left many descendants in Fredonia and other parts of Chautauqua County. A great-grandson, William Moore, now living in Fredonia. In 1915, Nelson Moore, aged 84 years, son of King Moore, was living at Lincoln, Neb., and was said to have been the only real son of a Revolutionary soldier at that time living in the United States west of Chicago. He was born at Fredonia when the soldier of the Revolution was in his sixty-eighth year.

MUNSON, SAMUEL—Born at Farmington, Conn., July 9, 1762. Died at Portland, Chautauqua County, N. Y., Feb. 27, 1841. Grave in Portland Cemetery. Enlisted at Southington, Conn., 1778, under Capt. Woodruff and Col. Stooker. Enlisted 1779, under Capt. Hodges, Col. Russell. Enlisted 1779 under Capt. Goodrich, Col. Myer Skidmore. Enlisted 1781 under Capt. Woodruff, Col. Myer Skidmore. Enlisted 1782 under Capt. Woodruff, Col. Sanford. Married Martha Barnes at Hartford, Conn., Feb. 3, 1784. She died in Portland, Dec. 6, 1845. He is mentioned in the Pension List of 1840.

PARKER, SAMUEL—No record of birth or death. Grave supposed to be in Cemetery, town of Portland. Supposed to have been a soldier of the American Revolution. No record of personal or military history has been found.

PETERS, JOSEPH PHELPS—Born at Hebron, Conn., Nov. 7, 1761. Died at Portland, Chautauqua County, N. Y., Sept. 21, 1843. Grave in Portland Cemetery. Enlisted at Hebron, Conn., in April,

BENJAMIN PRESCOTT CHAPTER, FREDONIA, N. Y.

1776, under Bissell Phelps. Second enlistment May, 1779, under Squire Hill, Col. McClellon. Third enlistment April, 1780, under Lieut. Wales. Married Azuba Case in Vermont, in 1784. Married Lydia Day at Pittstown, N. Y., April 8, 1794. They came to Portland in 1825. Son by first wife died in 1801. Children by second marriage: Azuba, Joseph, David, Lydia, John, Eliza. He was a pensioner and is mentioned in the Pension List of 1840.

POTTER, Capt. JEREMIAH—Born in Rhode Island, April 17, 1765. Died August 12, 1812. Grave supposed to be in Portland Cemetery. No authentic record of his military service has been ascertained, although he is credited with having served in the Revolutionary war and attained the rank of Captain. He married Polly Barnes in Herkimer County, N. Y., Nov. 9, 1799. In 1810 he became a settler of the town of Portland, Chautauqua County, N. Y.

PHELPS, JONATHAN—Born in Lyme, Conn., Feb. 1, 1763. Died at Fredonia, N. Y., Sept. 26, 1857. Grave in Fredonia Cemetery. Enlisted at Lyme, Conn., in March, 1781, under Capt. Ely. Second enlistment in May, 1782, under Capt. Morgan and Col. Wells. Third enlistment, 1783, under Capt. Comstock, Col. Wells. Was married to Charity Beckwith, at East Haddam, Conn., Aug. 14, 1784. Was granted pension and is mentioned in the Pension List of 1840. He enlisted four times, the last time in 1783, under Capt. Burnham and Col. Wells, and he became a mariner on the Privateer "Marshall." Was at the siege of Yorktown.

RISLEY, ELIJAH—Born in Connecticut, Dec. 1, 1757. Died in Fredonia, N. Y., Jan. 11, 1839. Grave in Fredonia Cemetery. No record of his military service has been obtained, but family records show he was granted pension for service as Revolutionary soldier. His wife was Phoebe Bill, born 1761. They moved from Cazenovia, N. Y., to Fredonia in April, 1807, and settled on the west side of Canadaway Creek where he built a grist mill. They had 12 children, of whom 9 attained majority, some of the descendants now living in Pomfret.

ROOD, JEREMIAH—Born at Lebanon, Conn., in 1753. Died in 1830. Grave in Fredonia Cemetery on lot of his cousin, Joseph Rood. He served as private with Connecticut troops in the Revolutionary war, was awarded a pension for his services and is mentioned in the Pension List of 1818 as residing in Chautauqua County, N. Y.

ROOD, JOSEPH—Born May 7, 1750, at Lebanon, Conn. Died at Fredonia, Chautauqua County, N. Y., March 31, 1843. Grave in Fredonia Cemetery. About April 19, 1775, responded to the call of Lexington, marched to Boston in the command of Capt. Joseph Hill, remained about a week and returned home. Soon after was called to New York when his brother, Jeremiah, who had enlisted, was called to New York. The illness of another brother and the infirm condition of the father caused Joseph to remain at home for a time and he then hired a substitute to take his place in the army, paying him $119. A few months later the improved condition of his brother at home enabled Joseph to volunteer to go to Roxbury in Capt. Jeremiah Mason's Company where he served three months and assisted in erecting forts on Dorchester Hill. He witnessed the evacuation of Boston. At Roxbury he had his right arm injured, was carried home and confined to the house for about four weeks. He next enlisted in the Company of Capt. Stephen Palmer, went to Providence and shortly after was taken ill with

19

fever and returned home. He remained at home until the alarm of the burning of New London when he joined the Company of Capt. Daniel Durham, remaining in the service a few weeks. He came to Pomfret, Chautauqua, N. Y., about 1816, in company of Elijah Risley. Applied for pension in 1838, and as he knew of no one who could prove his services, his brother Jeremiah having died about 8 years previous, he refers to Rev. Lucius Smith, Doct. Squire White, Gen. Leverett Barker, Gen. Elijah Risley, Col. Thos. G. Abel, Judge Benj. Walworth, Judge Whilo Orton, Judge Zattu Cushing, Jacob Houghton, Esq., John Walker, Esq., Frances H. Ruggles, John Cram, Esq., Major Henry Bosworth, Major A. H. Walker, James Mullett, Esq.

SEAVER, ROBERT W.—Born at Worcester, Mass., July 3, 1762. Died at Charlotte, Chautauqua County, N. Y., July 31, 1836. Grave in Charlotte Cemetery. Enlisted in 1776, serving six years and eight months. Was with Washington's army and under Lafayette when Cornwallis surrendered. Received honorable discharge at end of war. His wife was Anna Edson. In the spring of 1809, he became the first white settler of Charlotte Center.

SEYMOUR, WILLIAM — Born at New Hartford, Conn., Nov. 15, 1754. Died in Fredonia, Chautauqua County, N. Y., Dec. 22, 1841. Grave in Fredonia Cemetery. Enlisted March 1, 1776, under Aaron Austin, Col. Burrell, Connecticut Militia. Second enlistment in April, 1777, under Capt. John Strong. Third enlistment in Aug., 1778, under Nehemiah Lawrence. Fourth enlistment in 1780 under Capt. John Thompson and Col. John McCrea, serving until the fall of 1783. He married Sarah Patrick, at Stillwater, N. Y., March 20, 1783. She was born Oct. 24, 1755. He was allowed a pension and is mentioned in the Pension List of 1840. After his death pension was allowed wife. She died March 22, 1847.

SHATTUCK, SAMUEL—Born at Deerfield, Mass., Sept. 18, 1741. Died Sept. 1, 1827, at Portland, Chautauqua County, N. Y. Grave in Portland Cemetery. Was a soldier in the old French and Indian war and also in the Revolution. Was at Bunker Hill, the battles of Bennington and others, and at the battle of Yorktown. Married Chloe Field, a daughter of Aaron Field. She died in Mass., 1781. Children: Samuel, Chloe, Sidney, Seth, Lydia, Jessie, Chester. All born in Greenfield, Mass.

SINCLAIR, SAMUEL—Born May 10, 1762, at Nottingham, N. H. Died Feb. 8, 1827, at Sinclairville, Chautauqua County, N. Y. Grave in Evergreen Cemetery, town of Charlotte. Enlisted at Barnstead, N. H., June 21, 1777, at the age of 15 years, as private in the Regiment of his uncle, Col. Joseph Cilley. At the same time, two of his brothers, Bradbury and John, became members of the same company. He served 3 years, receiving an honorable discharge June 20, 1780, and was afterward awarded a pension. Was at the battle of Saratoga, at Valley Forge, and with Sullivan's expedition against the Indians in 1779. His parents, Joshua Sinclair and Mary Cilley, were married in Scotland and came to America about 1753. Samuel was the fifth of nine children. February 8, 1786, he married Sally Perkins at Vassalboro, Me. They had 10 children. With his family he removed to Otsego County in 1795 and later to Eaton, Madison County, N. Y. His wife died at Eaton in 1804 and was buried there. In 1805 he married Fanny Bigalow Edson, widow of Obed Edson. She was born at New London,

Conn., April 7, 1777. They had seven children. In 1810 they removed from Madison County to Chautauqua County, settling in the unbroken wilderness of what is now the town of Charlotte, buying from the Holland Land Company 360 acres of land at the price of 20 shillings per acre. While residing in Madison County he was commissioned Major in the state militia and was ever afterward known as Major Sinclair. The village of Sinclairville was named after him and he was the first Supervisor of the towns of Charlotte, Gerry, Cherry Creek, and Ellington, serving six terms. His wife Fanny, died at Sinclairville, Jan. 12, 1852. Her grave is beside husband in Evergreen Cemetery.

SMITH, ISRAEL—Born about 1763. Died December 6, 1836, at Laona, town of Pomfret, Chautauqua County, N. Y. The Fredonia Censor, Dec. 28, 1836, gives notice of his death. Enlisted in May, 1781, to Sept., 1783, serving as private under Capt. Morris, Col. Herman Swift, Connecticut Militia. Applied for pension in 1818 while residing at Cazenovia, N. Y. Pension allowed. Was married April 21, 1809, to Elenor, (maiden name not stated) at Cazenovia, N. Y., where wife continued to reside after death of husband. She was allowed pension. They resided with their children in their later years.

SMITH, EBENEZER—Born at South Hadley, Mass., Oct. 4, 1734. Died in Stockton, Chautauqua County, N. Y., July 6, 1824. Grave in Stockton Cemetery. He became a soldier in the French and Indian war, helping to build a fort near his father's house to serve as a refuge in times of attack by the Indians. Enlisted as private, Sept. 23, 1777, under Capt. Enoch Chapin, Col. Elisha Porter's Reg't. Discharged Sept. 29, 1777. Later served in expedition to the Northern Department, marching 120 miles. Married Remember Ellis, July 1, 1750. Married Lucy Shepardson in 1796, who died 1808. Married Esther Harvey in 1809, who died in 1814. He was a Baptist minister, was ordained at the age of 19 and preached for seventy-two years.

STONE, ISAAC—Born about 1762. Date of death and location of grave not ascertained. Served as private with Massachusetts troops in the Revolutionary war, was granted a pension in 1831 while residing in Chautauqua County, N. Y., and is also mentioned in the Pension List of 1840 as residing in the town of Cherry Creek.

TAYLOR, REUBEN—Born at Colchester, Conn., Feb. 8, 1759. Died at Portland, Chautauqua County, N. Y., March 9, 1833. Grave in Portland Cemetery. Enlisted at Glastonbury, Hartford County, Conn., in Dec., 1775, under Capt. Samuel Wright, Col. Samuel Wyllys. Second enlistment, May, 1777, under Capt. Elsworth Wright, Col. Swift. Third enlistment, May, 1778, under Capt. Theodore Woodbridge, Col. Sherman. Fourth enlistment, March, 1779, under Capt. Branne, Col. Enos. Married Anna Skinner at Hebron, Conn. in 1784. She was born in Hebron, Conn., Oct. 7, 1763. Pension was continued to widow after his death. Came to Portland in 1815. She died May 3, 1842. Children: Parsons, Erastus, Jared, Anna, Joseph, Dolly, Reuben, Justin, Betsy, Almon.

THOMPSON, REUBEN—Born Sept. 5, 1762, at Gloucester, Rhode Island. Date of death not ascertained. Grave in Fredonia Cemetery. He enlisted at Charlton, Mass., June 17, 1778, as private under Capt. Danforth Flower, Col. Thomas Nixon, Mass. troops. Also served under Capt. Nicholas and Col. Holman. Second, served under Capt.

Fowler and Col. John Greaton, also under Capt. Alton and Col. Davis. Re-enlisted March 25, 1780, under Capt. Joseph Crocker and Col. Greaton, attaining rank of Fifer. Granted a pension and mentioned in the Pension List of 1840 as residing in the town of Pomfret, Chautauqua County, N. Y. Was married twice, no names or dates.

TUCKER, Capt. SAMUEL—Born in Worcester County, Mass., May 10, 1760. Died in Portland, Chautauqua County, N. Y., Oct. 14, 1832. Grave in Portland Cemetery. Enlisted in 1776, serving six years and attaining rank of Captain. Was present and stood in line at the hanging of Maj. Andre, also participated in some of the battles under Gen. Ethan Allen. Married Anna Logan, who was born in Conn., Nov. 2, 1770 and died in Westfield, 1852. Children: Samuel, Jr., Susannah, Anna, Orpha, David, Laura, Olive, Hiram, William, Harriet, George.

TURNER, ASA—Born at Watertown, Conn., June 14, 1765. Died Nov. 27, 1847, at Stockton, Chautauqua County, N. Y. Grave in Stockton Cemetery. Enlisted March, 1778, at Harwinton, Conn., serving six months under Capt. Gillett. Second enlistment in 1779, under Capt. Howett and Col. Canfield. Third enlistment under Capt. Fenn, Col. Hopkins. Fourth enlistment in 1780 under Capt. Seldon, Col. Starr. Fifth enlistment in 1781 under Capt. Gideon Granger, Col. Wells. Sixth enlistment, 1782, under Capt. Jabez Fitch, Col. Wells. He became a Baptist minister, preaching many years at Pleasant Valley, N. Y. Name of wife not ascertained but at time of death was living with daughter, Louisa Jones, in Stockton. Is mentioned in the Pension List of 1840.

WALKER, LEWIS—Born in Connecticut in 1755. Died at Brocton, Chautauqua County, N. Y., in 1826. Location of grave not known. Served as private in Capt. Elnathan Nichols' Company, Major Starr's 3rd Conn. Reg't of Light Horse. He married Sarah Gunn who was born in 1761 and died in 1845. A daughter, Abigail, married Joshua Jackson.

WEBSTER, ELISHA—Born at North Bolton, now Vernon, Conn., son of Ezekiel and Chloe Elsworth Webster. Date of birth not known. Grave in Webster Cemetery, town of Pomfret, Chautauqua County, N. Y. No record of military service ascertained but family records say he was a Revolutionary soldier. In 1810, in company with his mother, brother and sisters, he came to Pomfret. He married Catherine Butler, who was a sister of the officer who had command of the fort at Pittsburg, Pa., in 1812. The children of Elisha and Catherine Webster were: Adaline Catharine, born in 1810; Charles Frederick, born in 1812; Orrin Chandler, born in 1815; Lemuel Butler, born 1819; Maria Ada, born 1820; John Butler, born 1821.

WIARD, DARIUS—Born about 1756. Date of death and location of grave not ascertained. He served as private in Connecticut troops in the Revolutionary war, and was granted a pension in 1831, while a resident of Chautauqua County, N. Y. He is also mentioned in the Pension List of 1840, aged 83, and residing in the town of Cherry Creek.

WOOD, NATHAN—Born about 1760. Date of death and location of grave not ascertained. He served as private with New York troops in the American Revolution and is mentioned in the Pension List of 1831, aged 71 years, and residing in Chautauqua County. There is record of the death of Mary Ann Wood, daughter of Nathan Wood, aged 16 years, which occurred April, 1829, in the town of Pomfret.

Jamestown Chapter, D. A. R.
Jamestown, N. Y.

Regent: STELLA FLORINE BROADHEAD
Historical Committee: LUCY NORTON SHANKLAND
RHODA FOSTER ROOT
CARRIE STAPLES CADWELL
EURYDICE AMES WELLMAN

Soldiers of the American Revolution who at one time resided in, or whose graves are located in one of the towns of Busti, Clymer, Ellicott, Ellery, French Creek, Harmony, Kiantone, and part of the town of Chautauqua, Chautauqua County, N. Y.

ADAMS, WILLIAM—Born October 19, 1754. Died April 1, 1841. Grave supposed to be in cemetery in French Creek, Chautauqua County, N. Y. Enlisted in April or May, 1775, served as private in company of Captain Wm. King and under Cols. Fellows and Ward, in Massachusetts Reg't. Enlisted at Roxbury, Mass. Was in the battles of Long Island and Harlem Heights. Was severely wounded at the latter battle and unable to finish his term of enlistment. Pension granted him in May, 1818. Also mentioned in Pension List of 1840. He was married in 1787 to Anna Walters, or Waters, at Marlborough, Conn. They had nine children and two of their sons were killed in the war of 1812. Three of their children were: Taylor, born March 28, 1789, died Aug. 17, 1817; James, born April, 1806; Sally, born March, 1808. The family became residents of French Creek at an early part of the nineteenth century. After his death in 1841, his wife applied for pension which was granted in 1845. At that time she was 79 years of age.

ANNIS, JACOB—Born 1761. Died November 14, 1841, in the town of Ellery, Chautauqua County. N. Y. Grave supposed to be in Lewis Cemetery. Was a soldier in the American army, having enlisted about 1780, serving until the close of the war, as private under Captains Luke Hitchcock, Jesse Hollister, Sylvanus Smith and Col. Joseph Vose, Massachusetts Militia. Was at the battles of White Plains, King Bridge and the surrender of Cornwallis. He enlisted at Newbury, Mass., and applied for pension April 30, 1818, while residing at Lavonia, Ontario County, N. Y., at which time he was 57 years of age. Pension was granted and he was mentioned in the Pension List of 1840, aged 77 and residing in the town of Ellery, Chautauqua County, N. Y. He was married November 18, 1804, to Deborah, widow of William Underhill, at Avon, N. Y. His widow was allowed pension on application May 30, 1853, at which time she was 67 years of age. In 1854 she was residing with her son, George, at Eaton Rapids, Mich. In 1820 their children referred to were Polly, aged 15; Eliza, aged 12; Underhill, aged 11; Nabby, aged 8; Deborah, 6; Wright, 4; William, 2, and Morris, 5 months.

BABCOCK, JONATHAN—Born Dec. 8, 1762, at Stonington, Conn. Died May

16, 1842, aged 79 years and 5 months. Grave in Bemus Point Cemetery, town of Ellery, Chautauqua County, N. Y. Enlisted April 1, 1782, while residing at Stephentown, N. Y. Served as private under Captain Pearce and Col. Willet, New York troops. Discharged Dec. 31, 1782, at Fort Plain, N. Y. Granted pension in 1832 while residing at Burlington, Otsego County, N. Y. He is mentioned in the Pension List of 1840 as residing with Benjamin Parker in the town of Ellery, Chautauqua County, N. Y. His wife, Rebecca, died July 4, 1841, aged 78 years and 7 months. Her grave is beside husband in Bemus Point Cemetery.

BACON, LEMUEL—Born at Brimfield, Conn., 1764. Died October 6, 1844, aged 80 years. Grave in Bemus Point Cemetery, town of Ellery, Chautauqua County, N. Y. Served in American army, enlisted at Easton, Washington County, N. Y., May, 1778, served as private under Captain Martin and Col. Warner, New York state militia. Applied for pension February 17, 1834, while residing at Fort Ann, Washington County, N. Y. His claim was allowed and he is mentioned in the Pension List of 1840, residing with William Bacon in the town of Ellery, Chautauqua County, N. Y. His father was Joseph Bacon.

BARNEY, LUTHER—Born at Norwich, Conn., March 4, 1757. Died in the town of Ellery, Chautauqua County, N. Y., Sept 30, 1844. Grave in Bemus Point Cemetery. He was the youngest child of John Barney, who with his brother came to America from the north of England about 1720 and settled at Norwich, Conn. At the commencement of the American Revolution, Luther Barney became a "Minute Man," afterwards serving as private in Captain Jesse Huntington's Company, Col. Selden's Reg't, Connecticut Militia. During the battle of Bunker Hill he was stationed at Roxbury, Mass., and was with the troops of Connecticut formed to reinforce Washington in the vicinity of New York, participating in the battle of Long Island and other engagements. On the expiration of his term of enlistment, after serving two years, he joined the American navy where he remained until the close of the war. While in the navy he and his brother Edwin were taken prisoners. Edwin died of small-pox on the prison ship, but Luther was afterwards exchanged and returned to his father's home in Norwich where he was shortly after married to Abigail Winship. They moved to Burlington, Vt., and afterwards to Genoa, Cayuga County, N. Y. His wife died in 1799 and was buried at Genoa. They had ten children: Sophia, William-Pitt, Charles, Philemon, Joseph, Luther, Nathan, Betsey, William, Samuel. About 1800 he married his second wife, Ruth Garrison, who was born in a fort in Maryland, Jan. 24, 1777. Their children were Sally Maria, Lysander, Ai, Benjamin, Alva, Zee, Milo, Anna, Clark, Ruth. In 1813 they moved to Newstead, Erie County, N. Y., where they remained until 1831 when they moved to Chautauqua County, making their home in the town of Ellery. He applied for pension in 1832, which was granted, and he is mentioned in the Pension List of 1840. His wife, Ruth, died Oct. 16, 1848, and is buried beside her husband in the Bemus Point Cemetery. Ruth, the youngest of his 20 children, married Charles G. Maples, for many years prominent in the official and business affairs of the County. She was a "Real Daughter" of the Revolution and at the time of her death in 1901 was a member of Patterson Chapter, D. A. R., Westfield, N. Y.

BEEBEE, AMON—Born in 1751. Died at Clymer, Chautauqua County, N. Y., February 21, 1830. Grave supposed to be in Clymer Cemetery. Was a soldier in American Revolution, serving as private with Massachusetts troops. Is mentioned in the Pension List of 1830 as residing in Chautauqua County.

BEMUS, WILLIAM—Born Feb. 25, 1762, in Saratoga County, N. Y. Died January 2, 1830, aged 67 years, 10 months, 7 days. Grave in Bemus Point Cemetery, town of Ellery. He served as private in Capt. Ephriam Woodworth's Company, under Col. Cornelius Van Veghten's Reg't, Albany County, New York Militia. He emigrated to Chautauqua County in the year 1805 and settled at the "Narrows" on Chautauqua Lake, in the spring of 1806, afterwards known as Bemus Point. He was united in marriage to Mary Prendergast in 1782. She was the eldest daughter of William Prendergast and sister of James and Mathew Prendergast, both of whom were prominent in the early affairs of Chautauqua County. She died July 11, 1845, aged 85 years. Her grave is beside her husband.

BENEDICT, SAMUEL—Born July 29, 1753, at Danbury, Conn. Died June 28, 1845, aged 92 years. Grave in Ashville Cemetery, town of Harmony. He served in Col. Philip Bradley's Battalion, Wadsworth Brigade, also in Capt. Reuben Scofield's Company, Connecticut Militia. He is mentioned as a pensioner in the census of 1840, aged 87, residing with William Dean in the town of Harmony. His wife, Sarah, died March 17, 1845, aged 90 years, and is buried beside him.

BOYD, JOSEPH—Born Nov. 5, 1759. Died March 19, 1846. Grave in Lewis Cemetery, town of Ellery. Enlisted in April, 1780 or 1781, served as private under Captains Clift and Hart and Col. John Durkee, Connecticut Militia. Was at the battle of Yorktown and the surrender of Cornwallis. Residence at time of enlistment, Plainfield, Conn. Applied for pension in April 1818. Claim allowed. Residence at that time was Brookfield, Madison County, N. Y. He is mentioned in the Pension List of 1840 as residing in the town of Ellery, aged 81 years and residing with Alvin Boyd. He was married Feb. 5, 1784, to Zerna Williams, who was born Oct. 10, 1760. Their children were: James, Martin, Zilpha, Alvin, Susanna, Lucretia.

CAMPBELL, JOHN—Born January 31, 1762, at Abington, Plymouth, Mass. Died Sept. 2, 1851, aged 89 years, 7 months. Grave in Clymer Cemetery, town of Clymer, Chautauqua County, N. Y. The records of the Pension Department at Washington show that while a resident of Norton, Bristol County, Mass., he enlisted Dec. 1, 1776, served 3 months as private in Capt. Clapp's Company, Col. Daggett's Massachusetts Reg't and was in several skirmishes. He enlisted Jan. 2, 1778, as private in Capt. Jacob Fuller's Company, Col. John Jacobs' Mass. Reg't, was in Sullivan's Expedition and in the battle of Rhode Island and was discharged Jan 1, 1779. He enlisted at Lyme, New Hampshire, March 1, 1781, and served one month as Orderly Sergeant in Capt. Nelson's New Hampshire Company. He enlisted July 10, 1781, served as Corporal 3 months and 27 days in Capt. Jabez Barney's Company, Col. Drury's Mass. Reg't. He enlisted at Beverly, Mass., in Sept., 1782, on board the privateer "Mohawk," Captain Carnes, was taken prisoner shortly after when the ship was captured by the British ship "Enterprise" and was held a prisoner about six and one half

25

months until after peace was declared, when he was released. He was allowed a pension Oct. 1, 1834, while a resident of Ticonderoga, N. Y. He is mentioned in the Pension List of 1840, residing at Clymer. He was on the pension rolls at Albany and it is said that each year he was paid his pension in silver dollars. Most of his family life was spent at Ticonderoga, N. Y. He came to Clymer, Chautauqua County, about 1838, and after the death of his wife in 1847, made his home with his daughter, Electa Campbell Beecher, in Clymer. He was locally known as "Captain" John Campbell, altho there is no record he held the office of Captain in army or navy. His wife, Abigail, rests by his side in the Clymer Cemetery and on the stone is inscribed: "Abigail, wife of John Campbell, died Sept. 11, 1847, aged 78 years, 10 months and 6 days. Blessed are the dead who die in the Lord." A son, Vincent Campbell, is buried beside them in the Clymer Cemetery. A daughter, Betsey Moses, was living in Clymer in 1856.

CHAMBERLAIN, PHINEAS—Born in Hopkinton, Middlesex County, Mass., Sept 11, 1760. Died March 22, 1847, aged 86 years. Grave in Town Line Cemetery. town of Harmony. He enlisted at Hopkinton, Mass., served under Captains Moore and Winchell and Cols. Herrick and Brown. Was at the battles of Lake George and the Surrender of Burgoyne. Applied for pension June 26, 1833, while a resident of Harmomy, Chautauqua County. He was united in marriage in 1791 to his wife Rebecca. Her death occurred May 12, 1854, aged 88 years, 10 months. She was allowed pension after her husband's death. He is on the pension List of 1840.

CHENEY, EBENEZER — Born at Orange, Mass., Sept. 7, 1761. Died Aug. 12, 1828, aged 66 years, 11 months and 26 days. Grave in Kiantone Cemetery, town of Kiantone. In company with his uncle, John Jones, he enlisted in April, 1775, at Mendon, Mass., as "Minute Man" in Captain Geninson's Company, third Reg't of Worcester County, Mass., Col. Tyler commanding. Both continued in service until the end of the war and were with Washington's army during the various engagements in the vicinity of New York, spent the winter of intense suffering at Valley Forge, and witnessed the surrender of Cornwallis. The father of the subject of this notice was also named Ebenezer Cheney, born 1741, served as a soldier in the Colonial army under Gen. Wolf, was at the battle of the Plains of Abraham and the taking of Quebec, and his father was a soldier in the old King Philip war at Mendon in 1666. Ebenezer Cheney married Anna Nelson, at Milford, Mass., February 17, 1785. She was the daughter of Seth Nelson and Silence Cheney. Her death occurred Nov. 10, 1835, and her grave is beside husband in Kiantone Cemetery. Their children were: Ruby, Polly, Nelson E., Levi, Anna, Abigail, Maria. With his family Ebenezer Cheney came to Chautauqua County in the winter of 1813, from Dover, Vt. With all their family possessions, and one team of horses and one of oxen, it required thirty days to make the journey. It was cold weather and they were obliged to seek shelter wherever night overtook them. When they arrived in Buffalo, they found the roads badly drifted with snow and were obliged to travel some of the way on the ice on Lake Erie. Finally arriving in Chautauqua County, they proceeded to the home of their daughter, whose husband was William Sears and who had opened a log tavern in the town of Carrol. In a short time they had selected the land for their future home and built a log house, although they decided the first duty was to hew out some sap troughs and attend to the necessary work of making some maple sugar.

CLEVELAND, GARDNER—Born at Pomfret, Conn., Sept. 25, 1763. Died April 22, 1851, aged 88 years. Grave in Cemetery at Clymer, Chautauqua County, N. Y. He enlisted at Pomfret, Conn., Jan. 1, 1781, served as private in Capt. Elisha Hopkins' Company, Col. Samuel Webb's Connecticut Reg't, was transferred to Capt. Lemuel Cliff's Company, under Col. Alexander Hamilton, was at the siege of Yorktown, after which he returned to Col. Swift's Connecticut Reg't. Was discharged in October, 1783. Was granted a pension in 1832 while a resident of Clymer, and is mentioned in the Pension List of 1840. He, with his brother John, was one of the first settlers of the town of Clymer, 1820, and the first town-meeting was held in his house in 1821. His wife, Mary Holmes, died Feb. 8, 1830, in the 65th year of her age. They had three children: John, born in 1788, married Eunice Fitch; Gardner, Jr., born 1790, married Lydia Parkhurst; Roxanna, born 1793, married William F. Brown. On May 7, 1832, Gardner Cleveland married Huldah Deming at Portland, N. Y. She was allowed pension after his death. In 1860 she was living in Illinois. Grave of his wife Mary is by his side in Clymer Cemetery.

COE, JOHN—Born Sept. 20, 1757 or 1758, at Southbury, Conn. Died Feb. 19, 1846, at Ellery, N. Y., aged 89 years and 5 months. Enlisted in American army at Southbury, Conn., in June, 1776, served as private in company of Capt. Rogers, Col. Gay's Reg't. Re-enlisted in Dec., 1776, again in 1777, 1778, 1779, 1780 and in 1781, serving under Captains David Hinman, Curtis and Johnson and Cols. Hinman and Preston, Connecticut Militia. The last six months of his service he was teamster. He applied for pension Feb. 13, 1834, while a resident of Ellery, Chautauqua County, N. Y. Pension was granted. He is also mentioned in the Pension List of 1840. His first six month's service in the army was as substitute for his brother Andrew. Captain David Hinman, in whose Company he was attached, was his grandfather. John Coe was united in marriage April 23, 1781, at Southbury, Conn., to Lois Johnson. She was born Oct. 12, 1762. They had the following children: Noble, Albert, Hadazsah, Alvin, Sabrina, Matilda, John, Warren, Henry, Lois Ann. The son Henry is mentioned as living in the town of Ellery in 1850. The wife of John Coe, Lois, was granted a pension April 18, 1848, at which time she was residing in the town of Ellery. She died Aug. 27, 1851. Warren J. Coe, son of John Coe, was born July, 1800, and died March, 1857. And Henry Coe, son of John Coe, was born June 17, 1803, and died Nov. 16, 1887. The graves of the latter are in the Oregon Cemetery, town of Stockton. They left many descendants. The graves of John Coe and wife are in "Red Bird" Cemetery, town of Ellery.

COMSTOCK, MARTIN L.—Born Aug. 1, 1757. No record of the time of his death or location of his grave. Residence at time of enlistment, Warren, Litchfield County, Conn. That place was the home of his parents. Enlisted Jan. 5, 1776, served as private under Capt. Beebe and Col. Ward, Connecticut Militia. Enlisted May 6, 1776, to Jan., 1777, served under Capt. Ebenezer Couch and Col. Herman Swift. He re-enlisted in 1777 and again in 1778 and 1779, serving under Captains Carter,

Sturdevant, and in the regiment of Col. Canfield. Date of application for pension, October 9, 1833, at which time he was a resident of Busti, Chautauqua County. He is mentioned in the Pension List of 1840 as living in Busti. He referred to his wife when he made application for pension but the location of their graves is not known. His father was Abel Comstock, of Warren, Conn.

COVEL, BENJAMIN—Born 1761 at Harwich, Mass. Died Nov. 22, 1822, in the town of Carroll, Chautauqua County, N. Y. Grave supposed to be in the same town. He enlisted in the Continental army in 1777 and served during the remainder of the war. It is recorded that he was at the taking of Burgoyne, at Sullivan's defeat and at the battle of Monmouth. He was married in 1784 to Sibyl Durkee, in Washington, Conn. She died in 1831, aged 69, at Covington, N. Y. He moved to the town of Carrol, Chautauqua County, in 1810, where he died. His sons and daughters, and his brother Seth, were all residents of the same neighborhood and the settlement was called Covelton.

COWING, JOHN—Born about 1761. Died in the town of Ellicott, Chautauqua County, N. Y., in Aug., 1833. He served as private in Massachusetts troops in the war of the American Revolution. Was awarded a pension and is mentioned in the Pension List of 1831, aged 71 years, and residing in Chautauqua County. Location of grave not ascertained.

CRAWFORD, ANDREW—Born in 1761. Died May 28, 1839, aged 78 years. Grave in Lakeview Cemetery, Jamestown. He served as private in the Company of Captain Perez Graves, mustered at Hatfield, Mass., in response to the alarm of April 19, 1775, to Ware; service 2 days. Enlisted May 18, 1775, served under Capt. Israel Chapin, Col. John Fellows. Enlisted Jan. 1, 1777, served as private under Captain Ward and Col. Weston until Jan 1, 1780. Discharged Dec. 6, 1780. Applied for pension, April 13, 1818, at which time he was residing at Sullivan, Madison County, N. Y., aged 57 years. In 1820 he referred to his wife name not stated, aged 55 years.

DAVIS, SAMUEL—Born in 1756 in Massachusetts. Died December 26, 1834, aged 78 years. Grave in Magnolia Cemetery, town of Chautauqua. Served as a drummer, from Stockbridge, Mass., with the "Minute Men" at Lexington, and as drum-major in 1780 under Captain John Chadwick. Was united in marriage with Ruth Holley of Lee, Mass. Their daughter, Temperance Kennedy Davis, married Thomas Whitney of Stockbridge, Mass., Jan. 23, 1814, and their son, Isaac Davis, married Roxalany Wilson.

DELAMATER, BENJAMIN—Born June 1, 1762, at Amenia, Dutchess County, N. Y. Died April 26, 1832, at Jamestown, N. Y. Was buried in old Cemetery at Jamestown. Body later removed to Lakeview Cemetery, but location of grave unknown. He served in Capt. Marshal's Company, Col. Willett's Reg't, Levies, N. Y. state Militia, for the term of nine months in the year 1781. Record on file in Comptroller's office, N. Y. state Revolutionary Records, vol. 4, folio 1, page 4. He was the son of Johannes and Maria Kipp Delamater, and had a twin brother, Jacob. Married Sarah Gifford, daughter of Capt. Roland Gifford of Chatham, N. Y. Wife died leaving one daughter. The latter died at the age of 10 years. About 1794 he married Isabel Beverly of Florida, N. Y. Moved to Jamestown,

N. Y., in the early part of the 19th century. His wife, Isabel, died Aug. 22, 1846. Their children were, Benjamin, John, Maria, Betsey, Thomas Jefferson, George Clinton, Caroline, Jacob, Mary Ann.

DIX, JOSEPH—Born at Leicester, Mass., July 7, 1753. Died Sept. 16, 1822, aged 69 years. Grave in Lake View Cemetery, City of Jamestown. He was the son of Joseph and Sarah Chubbs Dix, Sturbridge, Mass. He enlisted in the American army at Sturbridge, was one of the "Minute Men" at the battle of Lexington, served as private, and afterwards promoted to Corporal and Sergeant, was in Capt. Martin's Company, also in Capt. Timothy Perkins' Company, Col. Warren's Reg't and Col. Bigelow's Reg't. Discharged from service March 10, 1780. Was granted pension. Married Sarah Fisher, of Sturbridge, Mass., and early in the 19th century they emigrated to Western New York, settling in Jamestown about 1814 or 1815. He erected and operated a saw mill for some years, and when the Congregational Church of Jamestown was organized in 1816 he was elected its first deacon. The following is a tablet placed in that church to his memory: "In memory of Joseph Dix, who died in 1822, one of the Founders of this Church and it's First Deacon. He served 5 years in the Revolutionary war. The memory of his service to Church and Country is an enduring blessing."

ELY, WILLIAM—Born at Haddam, Conn., 1752. Died April 6, 1838. Location of grave not ascertained. Served as private in Connecticut Militia in the war of Revolution. Was granted pension in 1818 at which time he was residing in Chautauqua County, N. Y. His service was under the command of Capt. John Ventrix, Conn. troops. He married Hannah Barker. A daughter, Olive, was born in 1783.

FENTON, ADONIJAH—Born 1754. Died February 4, 1844, aged 90 years. Grave in Magnolia Cemetery, town of Chautauqua. Enlisted May, 1775, at Connecticut, served 3 years and 6 months, with rank of Corporal and Sergeant. Date of application for pension, April 15, 1818, at which time he was residing at Oneida County, N. Y. Claim allowed. He is mentioned in the census pension list of 1840 as aged 86 and residing with Henry Whitney in the town of Chautauqua. He married Drusilla Hinckley, of Westmoreland, N. Y., who was born 1768. Their daughter, Aurelia Fenton, born at Willington, Conn., Aug. 11, 1794, married Henry Whitney, a brother of Thomas Whitney, who was a son-in-law of Samuel Davis, Revolutionary soldier. In 1820, his wife was 52 years of age and a son, Lathrop, 10 years of age. His wife preceded him in death and at his death in 1844 he left the following children: Amariah, of Jackson, Washington County, N. Y., and Ambrose of Windsor, Ohio.

FENTON, JACOB—Born 1765 at Mansfield, Conn. Died Jan. 21, 1822 at Fluvanna, Chautauqua County, N. Y., aged 58 years. Grave in Fluvanna Cemetery. He enlisted in the Continental army at about the age of 15 years and served during the remainder of the war. Was a pensioner. Was a brother of Nathaniel Fenton. Was married to Lois Hurd of New Milford, Conn., Sept. 13, 1790. Eight children were born to them. Moved to Mayville in 1812 and to Jamestown in 1813, and in the year 1817 took up their residence at Fluvanna, town of Ellicott, where he died. His wife died Nov. 11, 1845, aged 76 years. Grave beside husband.

29

FISH, CYRUS—Born in 1762. Died January 25, 1816, aged 54 years. Grave in Lake View Cemetery, Jamestown, N. Y. His home was at Stonington, Conn., and at the age of 16 years, according to the records of the Adjutant General's office of Connecticut, he enlisted Jan. 28, 1778, serving as drummer in Capt. Stanton's Company until July 1, 1779. On page 242, "Revolution Lists and Returns," Connecticut, it says: "Cyrus Fish, rank Fifer, term engaged for three years; town engaged for, Stonington, commencement of service, 1st January, 1780, expiration of term of service, 1st January, 1781. In the First Company, Col. Samuel B. Webb's Reg't." After the war he married Bridget Jones at Groton, Conn. Her death occurred Jan. 17, 1819, aged 51 years. Her father was said to have been one of the soldiers at Lexington. Cyrus Fish and family moved to Jamestown in 1814. He never recovered from the sickness developed in the army and died two years after coming to Jamestown, followed by the death of his wife in 1819. They left a large family. Their son, Cyrus, Jr., built a mill on the Cassadaga, and shortly after moved to Iowa where he died. Maria Fish, daughter, became the wife of Henry Baker, one of the prominent early residents of Jamestown. One of the daughters of Cyrus Fish, Jr., married Daniel Williams of Ashville; another married Dr. G. W. Hazeltine; one married Elijah Akins; one married Jesse Landon.

FRANK, LAWRENCE—Born 1747 at Frankfort, N. Y. Died April 6, 1813, at Busti, N. Y., aged 65 years, 7 months and 6 days. Enlisted in the Continental army and served in Col. Van Rensselaer's Reg't. Was taken prisoner by the British and confined aboard a ship in New York harbor for a time. During the earlier French and Indian wars as a child he was captured by the Indians and taken to Canada, where he remained about 3 years, according to family traditions. Mary Myers was the maiden name of his wife. He settled in Busti about 1811. The graves of both are in Frank Settlement Cemetery, town of Busti.

GRIFFITH, JEREMIAH—Born July 28, 1758, at Norwich, Conn. Died June 10, 1842, aged 83 years and 10 months. Grave in Fluvanna Cemetery, town of Ellicott. He enlisted in the American army in 1775 and served for five months as private in the company of Captain Hezekiah Baldwin, Connecticut Militia. Re-enlisted and served under Capt. Beebe, Connecticut Militia, for six months, and again in 1776 under Capt. Link Hanford, and in 1777 was on the northern frontier in the winter campaign in Canada. Again re-enlisted and served in 1778 under Capt. Hamcrack, N. Y. state Militia. At the time of his application for pension, which was granted, he was 68 years old, and it is recorded that he made the trip from Griffith's Point, Chautauqua County, N. Y., to Washington, D. C., on horseback. In February, 1806, with his wife and six children, and all his family possessions stowed away on a wood-sled, drawn by oxen, he took up his line of march from Madison County, N. Y., for the west. He reached Chautauqua in due time and leaving his wife and children at Mayville proceeded down the east shore of Chautauqua Lake where he found William Bemus who had made a settlement near what is now known as Bemus Point. On the advice of Bemus he decided to settle at the place now known as Griffith's Point. At that time it was an unbroken wilderness from that section to Warren, Pa. Returning to Mayville he started with his family down the lake side and were for a time lost in a blinding snow storm, but finally reached the log cabin of Wm. Bemus. The next day they all started for Griffith's Point, and in three days' time had erected a log house. He married Mary Crapsey, or Cropsey, who was born Feb. 8, 1764. They had six children, John, Seth, Samuel, Polly, Jeremiah, and Alexander. He is mentioned in the Pension List of 1840, aged 82, residing with A. Griffith in the town of Ellery.

HAZELTINE, DANIEL—Born at Mendon, Mass., Dec. 20, 1761. Died June 26, 1828, aged 67 years. Grave in Lake View Cemetery, city of Jamestown. He enlisted in the Continental army Oct. 27, 1779, and was discharged April 22, 1780. Service 5 months and 25 days. He was a private in Capt. Ephriam Hartwell's Company, stationed at Rutland. His wife, Susanna Jones, was born at Milford, Mass., Sept. 25, 1766. She died June 22, 1852. They left many descendants who became prominent in the affairs of Chautauqua County.

HOLLISTER, DAVID—Born 1755. Died July 15, 1843, aged 88 years. Grave in Ashville Cemetery, town of Harmony. He enlisted in 1775 in Captain Hubbard's Company, and Col. Douglass' Reg't, Connecticut Militia, and afterwards served in Capt. Webb's Company and Col. Chester's Reg't. His third enlistment was in Capt. Smith's Company and Col. Talcott's Reg't. At the time of his first enlistment he was a resident of Glastonbury, Conn. Was granted a pension, at which time he was a resident of Delhi, N. Y. He was married January 26, 1780, to Sarah Goodrich. She was born in April, 1759, and after her husband's death, while a resident of Chautauqua County, was allowed a pension. He is mentioned in the Pension List of 1840, aged 86, and residing with Anson Phelps in the town of Harmony. His wife is buried beside husband.

IVES, ENOS—Born in the year 1759 at Walingford, Conn. Died in 1827 while residing in the town of Ellery, Chautauqua County, N. Y. Location of grave not known. Family records say he was one of the "Minute Men," who responded at the call of Lexington, serving in the Company of Captain John Couch, and that he was at Fort Washington when his captain and many of his company were taken prisoners. The maiden name of his wife was Ruth Bingham. His son, Almon Ives, was the first supervisor of the town of Ellery, serving from 1821 to 1827.

JONES, JOHN—Born 1744 at Mendon, Mass. Died in 1828 at Busti, N. Y., aged 84 years. Grave in Hazeltine Cemetery, Busti, N. Y. In company with his nephew, Ebenezer Cheney, he enlisted April 19, 1775, as a "Minute Man" in Captain William Gennison's Company, Col. A. Tyler, commanding, 3rd Reg't of Worcester County, Mass., and participated in the battles of Lexington, Concord and Bunker Hill. He re-enlisted in 1776, serving through out the war, was with Washington's army in the vicinity of New York, was at Valley Forge and witnessed the surrender of Cornwallis. His wife was Abigail Cheney, daughter of William Cheney of Mendon, Mass. He moved to Chautauqua County in 1810 and settled in the town of Kiantone. His wife died and was buried in Vermont. They had 7 sons and 4 daughters. One of the sons was Benjamin, with whom he lived in Kiantone. He was a deacon of the Kiantone Congregational Church.

31

DAUGHTERS of the AMERICAN REVOLUTION

LANDON, REUBEN—Born March 28, 1757, at Litchfield, Conn. Died Nov. 23, 1854, aged 97 years, 7 months and 25 days. Grave in Hatch Settlement Cemetery, town of Busti. The records in the Adjutant General's Office, Hartford, Conn., show that Reuben Landon served in the war of the Revolution in Capt. Alexander Waugh's Company, 17th Reg't, Connecticut Militia, and in July and August, 1779, under command of Lieut.- Col. Andrew Adams. He was married to Mary Way previous to 1779. He moved from Herkimer County, N. Y., to Busti, Chautauqua County, in the year of 1812, where he purchased land and resided until his death in 1854.

LOOK, ELIJAH—Born 1757. Died August 27, 1852, aged 95 years and 5 months. Grave in Pleasantville Cemetery, town of Chautauqua. On the headstone of his grave is the following inscription: "Elijah Look, a soldier of the Revolution and of the Cross of Christ." He enlisted January 18, 1776, served under Capt. Nathan Smith and Col. Norton. His second enlistment was under Capt. William Foster and Col. Norton. It is of family record that he participated in the capturing of a British ship at Nantucket, also in re-capturing an American brig which was grounded at Martha's Vineyard. His wife, Mary, died March 12, 1844, aged 78 years. Her grave is beside her husband. Their son, William R. Look, born 1799, died 1869. He was on the Pension List of 1840.

LOOMIS, SIMON—Born at Tolland, Conn., in 1756. Died at Blockville, in the town of Harmony, Chautauqua Co., N. Y., Nov. 26, 1842, aged 86 years. Grave in Blockville Cemetery. In 1775 served as private in 3rd Conn. Reg't under Capt. Experience Storrs and Col. Putnam. In 1777 commenced service in 2nd troop, Col. Sheldon's Light Dragoons. In 1779 in a detachment of Militia Horse, in command of Col. Seymour. It is of family record that he was with the troops of Washington at the crossing of the Delaware and also was at the battle of Yorktown and witnessed the surrender of Cornwallis. He was united in marriage with Mary Carpenter in 1787. They moved from Tompkins County, N. Y., about 1836, to Chautauqua County, settling in the town of Harmony where they had been preceded by a son, Daniel Loomis. Another son, Solomon Loomis, born 1796, married Hannah Armstrong. Mary, wife of Simon Loomis, died March 9, 1853, aged 84 years, and her grave is beside husband.

LOUCKS, JOSEPH—Born 1754. Died April 20, 1825. Grave in Fluvanna Cemetery, town of Ellicott. On the monument at Fluvanna Cemetery is inscribed the following: "Remains of J. and M. Loucks, settlers of the town in 1814." In 1814 he moved form Madison County, N. Y., to Chautauqua County, and settled in the south-east part of the town, with his sons John, Daniel, Hiram, and two daughters, Margaret, wife of Jeremiah Griffith, Jr., and Polly, wife of Wm. G. Youker. Later came the older sons, Joseph, Henry, Peter, and David, and a daughter, Charity, wife of John Rice, all whom had families or came with them. No record has been found of his military service, but he was locally known as a Revolutionary soldier.

MAPLES, JOSIAH—Born May 15, 1762, at New London, Conn. Died July 4, 1847, at Ellery, N. Y., aged 85 years, 1 month, 19 days. Grave in Cemetery at East Aurora, N. Y. It is recorded that he entered the American army at the age of 15 years and served in the Connecticut

32

Militia until ths close of the war. In 1782 he was united in marriage with Diadema Comstock, and in 1790 moved to Otsego County, N. Y. His wife died while residing in Otsego County and was probably buried in that county. In 1795 he married Esther Hedges, of New Jersey. In 1808 they moved to Milo, Yates Co., N. Y., and about 1826 moved to East Aurora, Erie County, N. Y. In the latter place he served some years as Justice of the Peace. His wife, Esther, died Sept. 27, 1831, aged 54 years and 6 months, while they were residing in East Aurora, and is buried by his side. In 1836 he moved to Chautauqua County and settled in the town of Ellery where he remained until his death. He was the father of 18 children all whom lived to have families of their own. His son, Charles G. Maples, was for many years prominent in the official and business affairs of the county. He is mentioned in the Pension List of 1840. Was a deacon of the Baptist Church.

MARSH, JASPER—Born 1759. Died April 30, 1841, aged 83 years. Grave in Stillwater Cemetery, town of Kiantone. Was a native of Massachusetts, enlisted in American army, Sept. and Oct., 1777, served as private in Captain Benjamin Freeman's Company, Col. John Holman's Mass. Reg't. Enlisted June 7th, 1778, in Worcester County, 10th Bat., Massachusetts Militia, under Col. Thomas Marshall, to serve 9 months, was discharged March 7th, 1779. Received pension from 1825 until his death in 1841. Was present at the surrender of Burgoyne. His wife was Submit Belden. Came to Kiantone, Chautauqua County, in 1811, where he followed the occupation of farmer and mechanic.

MARTIN, AARON—Born August 14, 1763. Died Feb. 18, 1842, aged 79 years. Grave in Stillwater Cemetery, town of Kiantone. He was born on Quaker Hill, Dutchess County, N. Y., son of Manassah and Sarah Martin, who settled there in 1747. It is of family record that he was a soldier in some of the later campaigns of the army in the Revolutionary war. He came to the town of Busti in the year 1811 and settled on lot 44 on the Stillwater. He was a tanner by trade. He married Mary Eggleston. She was born Jan. 10, 1764, died April 18, 1837. Grave beside husband in Stillwater Cemetery, Kiantone.

MARTIN, WILLIAM,—Born in Massachusetts, July 6, 1753. Died May 30, 1825, aged 72 years. Grave in Fluvanna Cemetery, town of Ellicott. The Centennial History of Chautauqua County says he was at the Battle of Bunker Hill, was under Arnold and Montgomery in the expedition against Quebec, where he was wounded. In 1780 he was one of the captives of the Indians at Little Falls, taken to Canada as a prisoner. After several months confinement he made his escape. He is mentioned in the pension list of 1818, residing in Chautauqua County, and as having served as private in Massachusetts Militia. His wife, Olive, died Sept. 30, 1833, aged 74 years. Her grave is beside husband. They left many descendants.

MATHER, NATHANIEL—Born at Lyme, Conn., May 20, 1759. Died Jan. 30, 1852, aged 92 years and 8 months. Grave in old Cemetery at Niobe, town of Harmony. It is related that at time of his enlistment in the American army of the Revolution he was residing at Lyme, Conn., and during his service was an aid to his uncle who was an officer. He is mentioned in the Pension List of 1840, of the town of Harmony, aged 81, and residing with Nathaniel Mather. It is

33

related that his wife never came to Chautauqua County and was buried at Lyme, Conn.

MATHEWS, THOMAS—Born April 9, 1748, at Westbury Society, New Haven County, Conn. Died Nov. 6, 1841. Grave probably in Old Cemetery, Jamestown, N. Y. Enlisted May 1, 1775, at Torrington, Conn., and served in the American army at intervals until May, 1778. Served under Captains Griswold and Gillet and Cols. Ainman, Sheldon, Canfield, Mead and Enos. Was at the battles of Forts St. John and Chanelby, Harlem. Residence at time of enlistment, Torrington, Conn. Made application for pension Oct. 4, 1832, while a resident of Penfield, Monroe County, N. Y. His claim was allowed. At that time he was living with a daughter. In the Pension List of 1840, his name appears as residing in the town of Ellicott, Chautauqua County, aged 93 years, and residing with Jabez Blackmar.

MATTESON, WILLIAM—Born Jan. 24, 1762. Died April 1858, aged 96 years. Grave on Connelly farm, near Stowe, overlooking Chautauqua Lake. He enlisted July 6, 1780, served until Dec. 12, 1780, and again enlisted Aug. 26, 1781, and served to Dec., 1781. His residence at time of enlistment was New London, Conn. Applied for pension Aug. 28, 1838, at which time he was a resident of the town of Harmony, Chautauqua County, N. Y. During his service in the Revolutionary war he served under Captains Elisha Heart, and Stephen Betts and in the Regiments of Colonels Wyllys and Herman Swift and Ebenezer Huntington, of the Connecticut Militia. It is said that he was the last surviving soldier of the Revolutionary war residing in Chautauqua County. He came from Otsego County, N. Y., in 1811, with his wife and 12 children and settled 3 miles from Ashville on the shore of Chautauqua Lake. One of his sons was the late Victor M. Matteson of Busti.

MOORE, ASA—Born June 29, 1762, at New Haven, Conn. Died at Kiantone, Chautauqua County, N. Y., Jan. 22, 1848, aged 86 years. His war record furnished by the Bureau of Pensions, claim S. 23817, says: "While residing at Windsor, Hartford County, Conn., he enlisted in March, 1778, and served one year as private under Lieut. Daniel Heyden or Hayden and Col. Roger Newberry in the Connecticut troops and was guarding the military and hospital supplies at Windsor. He enlisted in July, 1779, and served two months as private in Captain David Barber's Company, under Major Elihu Kent, Connecticut Troops. He enlisted in June, 1780, and served six months as private in Captain Abner Prior's Company, Col. Bradley's Connecticut Regiment. He was allowed a pension on his application executed Oct. 12, 1832, while a resident of Carroll, Chautauqua County, N. Y. Soldier stated that he and his family in 1794 or 1795 left Windsor, Conn., and moved to Wardsborough, Vermont, and in 1799 moved to New York State. In company with his friend, Eben Cheney, he came to Chautauqua County, N. Y., in the year 1812, and settled in the town of Kiantone, where he was later well known as Deacon Asa Moore. He is mentioned in the Pension List of 1840. His wife, Huldah King, was born in 1767 and died in 1840. Joseph K., their son, born in 1791, and died in 1872, was a soldier in the war of 1812. Their daughter, Amanda, born in 1793, died 1832. His wife is buried beside him in Kiantone Cemetery.

JAMESTOWN CHAPTER, JAMESTOWN, N. Y.

OSBORN, ISAAC—Born Sept. 19, 1760, at Wilbraham, Mass. Died Feb. 20, 1843, aged 82 years and 5 months. Grave in Cemetery, at Panama, town of Harmony, Chautauqua County, N. Y. While residing at Springfield, Mass., he enlisted Aug. 1, 1776, serving as private in Capt. John Bliss' Company, Mass. Militia, until Jan. 1, 1777. Enlisted in July, 1777, and served until Jan. 1, 1778, in Capt. John Morgan's Company, Mass. Militia. Enlisted in July, 1778, served six months in Capt. Enos Parker's Company, Mass. Militia. Enlisted Jan. 1, 1779, and served three years as an Artillery Artificer in Capt. William Barton's Company, under Lieut. Col. David Mason, at Springfield, Mass. Enlisted Jan. 8, 1782, and served to June 15, 1783 as Artificer in Capt. Hawes' Company, Col. David Mason's Reg't, Mass. Troops. Was allowed pension Oct. 12, 1832, while residing at Harmony, Chautauqua County, N. Y. In 1826 he referred to his wife, Anna, aged 66 years. He is mentioned in the Pension List of 1840, aged 79, and residing in the town of Sherman. His wife, Anna, died June 16, 1842, aged 83 years. Her grave is beside husband in Panama Cemetery. They were survived by two children, Levi and Lucy. The latter became the wife of Luke A. Patrick.

OWEN, JOHN—Born April 16, 1735. Died Feb. 24, 1843, while a resident of the town of Carroll, aged 107 years, 10 months and 8 days. He was a native of Winsor, Conn., was a soldier in the early French war and in the American army throughout the American Revolution. It is related that he was with General Wolf at Quebec in 1759 and with Col. Ethan Allen at Ticonderoga. He served as private in Captain Nathaniel Buels' Company, Col. Hinmans' Reg't, Connecticut Militia, May to Dec., 1775, as private in Capt. Roger Moore's Company, and Col. Fisher Gay's Reg't, Connecticut Militia, May to Oct., 1776, and July and Aug. 1777. And private in Captain Archelaus Buel's Company, Connecticut Militia, October, 1777. He came from the Susquehanna Valley, N. Y., to Warren, Pa., in 1806, and in 1808 located in the town of Poland, Chautauqua County, N. Y. In 1816 he sold his farm and located in the town of Carrol and at one time kept a tavern at Fentonville. He is mentioned in the Pension List of 1840 as residing with Reuben Owens in the town of Carrol. His grave is in the Warren, Pa., Cemetery. He was the maternal grand-father of the late Gov. Fenton of Jamestown. His wife, Lydia, who was born at Sunderland, Conn., Jan. 30, 1773, died Nov. 7, 1851, aged 78 years, 9 months and 8 days. Her grave is beside him in Warren Cemetery.

PALMITER, PHINEAS—Born in 1762 at Westerly, R. I. Died July 4, 1847. Location of grave not known. Enlisted at Hopkinton, R. I., served as private under Capt. Benjamin West, Captains Dickinson, Christopher Brown, Phineas Maxon, Nathan Adams, and Col. John Topham, R. I., Major Ledyard, Conn. He came to Chautauqua County in 1814 in company with his brother-in-law, Cyrus Fish. He applied for pension October 12, 1832, while a resident of Busti. He is mentioned in the Pension List of 1840, as a resident of the town of Busti and residing with John Palmiter.

PARKER, BENJAMIN—Born March 8, 1765, in Rhode Island. Died Nov. 7, 1842, aged 77 years and 8 months. Grave in Bemus Point Cemetery, town of Ellery. He was the son of Thomas and Jane Parker. At the early stage of the Revolution he was too young to enlist but during the latter part of the war he served for three years the Colonial government with an ox-team and cart as a transport. Jan. 7, 1788, he was united in marriage with Mary Davis at Hartford, Conn. She was a daughter of Ebenezer and Betsey Davis. They moved to Saratoga County, N. Y., and later to Washington and Otsego Counties, coming to Chautauqua County in 1816, locating in the town of Ellery where he purchased 120 acres of land, and where they continued to reside until his death. Their children were: Clark, Thomas, Phillip 1st, Phillip 2nd, Betsey Jane, Benjamin, George, Diantha, Amy, Ezekiel, Charles, Mary. Mary, wife of Benjamin Parker, died Jan. 26, 1847, in her 77th year. Her grave is beside husband.

PICKARD, JOHN—Born May 28, 1760. Died Aug. 30, 1827, aged 67 years, 3 months and 2 days. Grave in Red Bird Cemetery, town of Ellery. Enlisted at or near Johnstown, N. Y., 1779, and served in the Continental army under Captains Koch, Ruff and House, and in Col. Jacob Klock's Reg't N. Y. State Militia. Was captured by the Indians, on the Mohawk, near Little Falls, and kept a prisoner about 2 years. His father, Joseph Pickard, lived near Little Falls, N. Y. Was married at Herkimer, N. Y., Jan. 6, 1784, to Maria Margaret Garlock. She died March 26, 1851, and is buried beside her husband. Their children were: Charity, Stone, Peter, Nancy, Ludden, Sylvanus, Henry, Albert, Abraham, Magdalen, Adam, and Catharine. He became a resident of Chautauqua County, in 1816.

PIER, LEVI—Born June 3, 1754. Died in March, 1826, aged 72 years. Grave on Elias Jenner farm, town of Busti. He was a native of Great Barrington, Mass., and a grandson of Sergeant Thomas and Margaret Pier, who settled in Great Barrington in 1732. He served in the American army of the Revolution under Capt. Goodrich and was at the battle of Bennington. His wife, Ann Dewey, was born at Great Barrington, Mass., 1754, and died in Busti about 1816. Her grave is in Stillwater Cemetery, town of Kiantone. Levi Pier came from Oxford, N. Y., to Busti in 1814. He had 12 children: Elijah, Lois, Namah, Amasa, Sally, Abraham, Reuben, Oliver, Lovisa, Roxa, David.

RHODES, JOHN—Born in the year 1763 at Poughkeepsie, N. Y. Died about 1832. Grave in Fluvanna Cemetery, town of Ellery. Family records say he was a soldier in the American Revolution during 1777 and 1779, under Captains James Gray, Job Wright and Ephriam Woodworth, and was at the battles of Stillwater and Saratoga. New York State records credit him with service in 7th Regiment, Dutchess County Militia. His wife was Sybil Edmunds. Their son, Iram Rhodes, married Lydia, daughter of Daniel Deming.

SCOFIELD, SEELY—Born July 22, 1758. Died June 15, 1843, aged 84 years, 10 months and 23 days. Grave in Dewittville Cemetery, town of Chautauqua. He was the son of Sylvanus and Hannah Seely Scofield, of North Stamford, Conn. He enlisted in the Continental army at the age of 18 years and served six years and six months. He was a private in the Company of Captain Henry Ten Eyck's Light Infantry, Second Connecticut Reg't commanded by Col. Zebulon F. Butler; was also in Capt. Jonathan Whitney's Company, of Col. Mead's 9th Connecticut Militia; also served in Webb's Reg't under General Wooster, going to the latter's command after the battle of White Plains. He was married to Hannah Crissey, who was born March 24, 1766, at Stamford, Conn. With his family he moved to Saratoga County, N. Y., about 1795, remaining there until about 1800 when they moved to Onondaga County. He is mentioned in the Pension List of 1840 as living in the town of Ellery, Chautauqua County, at the age of 82, and residing with Haran Scofield.

SCOFIELD, WILLIAM—Born at Stamford, Conn., May 15, 1764. Died Sept. 26, 1851, at Ellery, N. Y. Grave in Lewis Cemetery, town of Ellery. He was 87 years and 4 months of age at the time of his death. He was the son of Josiah and Mary Smith Scofield. Enlisted in Fairfield County, Conn., in 1780, remaining in service until the close of the war, serving in Captain Hanford Hoyt's Company, Col. John Mead's Reg't, Connecticut Militia. His father, Josiah Scofield, also served as a soldier in the Revolution. William Scofield was united in marriage to Patty Seely, August 2, 1786. Their children were William and Patty. Wife died Dec. 7, 1789. Was married to Hannah Abbott Nov. 21, 1790. She died April 28, 1840. Her grave is beside husband. Their children were Smith and Polly. He came to Chautauqua County about 1820 locating in the town of Ellery, where he resided until his death in 1851. He left many descendants who have been prominent in the affairs of the county.

SMILEY, JOHN B.—Born May 18, 1763, in Donegal County, Ireland. Grave in Palmiter Cemetery, town of Busti. Date of death not known. When eleven years of age he came to America with his father's family. They located at Bedminister, N. J., where the son, John, enlisted in the American army in March, 1780, served until Jan. 1, 1781, as a teamster under Capt. John Davis, Col. Richard Butler, Pennsylvania Militia. Applied for pension in 1836 at which time he was residing in Busti, and he is mentioned in the Pension List of 1840 as residing with his son, Samuel Smiley, aged 79 years. His wife, whose maiden name was Mary Mott, died many years before he did, and is buried at Lansing, N. Y. They had a son, Samuel, and a daughter, named Matilda.

SMILEY, WILLIAM—Born in Connecticut, May 25, 1753. Died in Jan., 1825, aged 72 years. Grave in Fluvanna Cemetery, town of Ellicott, Chautauqua County, N. Y. He served in Capt. Stanley's Company, from Farmington, Conn., in Gay's Reg't, and, according to War Department records, his name appears in an account dated July 18, 1776, of the time of enlistment and marching of the men of that company to join the Continental army in New York, which shows he enlisted June 24, marched July 4 and joined the army July 7. He was united in marriage with Hannah Wilcox of Exeter, R. I., about 1780. She was born in 1760 and died in 1832 and is buried beside her husband. They had three children, Joseph, born Nov. 12, 1781; William, born May 25, 1783; Lucy, born April 7, 1785.

STAPLES, ISAAC—Born at Mendon, Mass., Nov. 23, 1764. Died at Jamestown, N. Y., May 23, 1848, aged 83 years and 6 months. Grave in Lake View Cemetery, city of Jamestown. Enlisted Feb. 8, 1781, for a term of 3 years in Capt. Amidon's Company, Col. Tyler's Reg't, Mass. Militia. Also as private in Capt. Joseph Killam's Company, Col. Rufus Putnam's Reg't. Was described at that time as "statue 5 feet, 5 in., complexion dark, occupation farmer." His wife, Esther

Benson Staples, was born in the year 1767 and died Aug. 31, 1855. Their children were: Pamelia, Anna, Phila, Sibbel, Abraham, Rocksey, Esther, Marinda, Scammel, Ira Franklin, Maria, Warren B., Fanny Minerva, Eveline. Marinda married Aaron Taylor, and Warren B., who was born 1803, married Fanny Cross. The wife of Isaac Staples was buried beside her husband in Lake View Cemetery.

STEARNS, Capt. WILLIAM—Born Aug. 5, 1754. Died Feb. 14, 1834, aged 79 years and 6 months. Grave in Stillwater Cemetery, town of Kiantone. He was a native of Worcester, Mass., son of Ebenezer and Mary Spring Stearns. He served in the American army during the Revolution, was a "Minute Man" and was at Boston at the time of the destruction of the British tea. He attained the rank of Captain and was present at many of the memorable events that occurred in the vicinity of Boston and was also at the battle of White Plains. His daughter, Lydia, became wife of Joseph Garfield. She was born at Orange, Mass., Dec. 14, 1784, died Sept. 15, 1851, aged 66 years. Grave in Stillwater Cemetery, Kiantone. Joanna, wife of Capt. William Stearns, was born Feb. 8, 1757, and died March 29, 1832, aged 66 years. They had 15 children: Franklin, Betta, Betta 2nd, Joanna, William, Jr., Lydia, Jonas, Simeon, Ebenezer, Dolley, Eloner, Amory, Mary, Joseph, and one child who died at birth.

STEDMAN, LEVI—Born in 1758. Died Oct. 26, 1834, aged 76 years. Grave in Pleasantville Cemetery, town of Chautauqua. His grave has a marker which is inscribed as follows: "Here lies the body of Levi Stedman, for 7 years and 8 months a faithful soldier of the Army of the Revolution. Died 26 October, 1834, aged 76 years." His wife, Anna, died June 27, 1857, aged 91 years, 2 months and 13 days. Her grave is beside husband. In the same cemetery are the graves of Levi Stedman, who died October 5, 1865, aged 72 years, and Amy, his wife, who died July 12th, 1867, aged 74 years, 3 months and 28 days. He is mentioned in Pension List of 1818, and was a private in Conn. Militia.

STEWARD, ELIPHALET — Born Aug. 14, 1759, at Stonington, Conn. Died November 3, 1837, aged 78 years. Grave in Lake View Cemetery, Jamestown. Enlisted in the American army in the fall of 1776, served 3 months as private under Capt. Jeremiah Halsey, Connecticut Militia. Enlisted in March, 1778, served one year under Captain Joseph Springer, Col. John Topham, Rhode Island Militia. Re-einlisted for one year as private in General Ezekiel Cornell's Life Guards, Rhode Island. Enlisted in Sept., 1782, served one month with rank of Lieut. in Reg't of Col. Vrooman, New York Militia. Was in Rhode Island battle. Was granted pension in 1832 at which time he was residing at Busti, Chautauqua County, N. Y. His wife, Mercy Coates, was born Sept. 5, 1764. They moved from Frankfort, N. Y., to Busti, Chautauqua County, in 1811. Her death occurred April 18, 1818. They had four children: Lucy, wife of Stephen Wilcox; John; Anna, wife of Walter Crouch; Betsey, wife of Michael Frank.

STOW, JOHN—Born 1763. Died Nov. 9, 1837, aged 74 years. Grave in Ashville Cemetery, town of Harmony. He was a native of Southboro, Mass., and, it is said, enlisted in the Continental army at the age of 17 years, serving as private and fifer. His wife was Sally Healey, and they had five sons and three daughters. The sons came to Chautauqua County in the early part of the 19th century and were followed by John Stow. He made his home with his eldest son, John Stowe, Jr., who was then residing in the town of Busti. His wife died Dec. 13, 1852, aged 84 years. Grave beside husband.

WASHBURN, WILLIAM—Born May 9, 1767, at Wendall, Mass. Died July 26, 1851. Was buried in the old Cemetery in Jamestown, and his body was later removed to Lake View Cemetery. He enlisted in the American army in March, 1781, serving as private until the close of the war in Capt. Killam and Hondin's Companies, and Col. Rufus Putnam's Reg't, Mass. Militia. Was granted pension in 1818 and is mentioned in the Pension List of 1840 as residing in the town of Ellicott, Chautauqua County. Was married in 1789 to Hulda Clark, who was born in 1768. Their children were: John C., Chelton, Erastus, Hannah, Luania. Erastus, who was born in 1798, married Judith Benson; Hannah, born in 1804, married Peleg Benson, and Luania married Saxon Benson. In 1822 he moved with his family to the town of Ellicott, Chautauqua County, N. Y. They left many descendants.

WATERBURY, SAMUEL—Born August 15, 1761. Died March 1, 1834. Grave in Pleasantville Cemetery, town of Chautauqua. Family records show that he had been a Revolutionary soldier and that he came from Saratoga County, N. Y., in 1810, and with Shadrack Scofield and David Waterbury, son of Samuel, made settlement in the southern part of the town of Stockton. Edson's History says that on December 31, 1812, at the home of Samuel Waterbury, in Stockton, John West and Martha Barnhart were united in marriage, which was the first marriage recorded in that town. Rachel Schofield, his wife, died Feb. 26, 1838, aged 79 years, 2 months and 26 days. Betsey Waterbury, daughter of Samuel and Rachel Waterbury, married Shadrach Scofield.

WELLMAN, BARNABUS—Born Aug. 15, 1756, at Killingsworth, Conn. Died March 7, 1847, aged 91 years. Grave in Wellman Cemetery, town of Busti. He served four years and eight months as Drummer and Drum-Major in the Revolutionary war. Enlisted at Killingsworth, Conn. Was in the Battles of White Plains, Trenton, Germantown and Monmouth. Applied for pension in 1818 while residing in Chautauqua County, and is mentioned in the Pension List of 1840, as aged 83 years and residing with his son, Homer Wellman, in the town of Busti. His wife, Lois Page, was born in 1761. They were married in 1780. Her grave is beside husband. They had the following children: James, born 1783; Homer, born in 1786, married Charlotte Lord, died 1858; Barnabus, born, 1793, married Pamela Bullock, died 1874; Ford, born 1796, married Sally Patchin, died 1830; Millie, born, 1791, married John Deming, died 1859; Hannah.

WELLMAN, JOHN—Born 1760. Died May 25, 1841, age 81 years. Residence at time of enlistment, Killingworth, Conn. Enlisted Jan. 3, 1777, served to Jan. 1780, as private under Captain Aaron Stevens and Col. Herman Swift, Connecticut Militia. Enlisted 1781, served as teamster under Capt. Ransom. Battles engaged in, Monmouth, and was at Valley Forge. Date of application for pension, April 13, 1818, claim allowed. Residence at date of application, Otsego County, N. Y. In 1820 was living at

Elba, N. Y. He was married May 12, 1787 to Phebe Tuttle on her 17th birthday. She was allowed a pension on her application executed March 20, 1845, while a resident of Chautauqua County. She died Dec. 9, 1854. He is mentioned in the Pension List of 1840 as living with William Blanchard in the town of Harmony, Chautauqua County, N. Y. They had the following children: John, Jr., Ira, Sally, Lydia, Barnabas, Stephen, Polly, Samantha, Oran, Philemon, Philander. The location of the graves of John Wellman, Sr., and his wife has not been ascertained.

WHITNEY, RICHARD, Sr.—Born Dec. 6, 1759, at Pittsfield, Conn. Died May 10, 1844, aged 84 years and 5 months. Grave in Magnolia Cemetery, town of Chautauqua. He was the son of Richard and Esther Clark Whitney. Enlisted at Lee, Berkshire County, Mass., in 1779, served 9 months as private under Capt. Miller and Cols. Brewer and Sprout. Residence at date of application for pension, Oct. 12, 1832, Chautauqua, Chautauqua County, N. Y. Claim allowed. He is mentioned in the Pension List of 1840 as residing at Chautauqua, aged 81 years. His wife, Ruth, died Dec. 28, 1851, aged 86 years, 7 months, 12 days. Grave beside husband. They had the following children: Henry, Electa, Thomas, Richard.

WILCOX, STEPHEN—Born in Rhode Island, Aug. 8, 1762. Died Sept. 15, 1846, aged 84 years. Grave in Wilcox Cemetery, town of Busti. Served as Corporal in Capt. Heacock's Company, from Dutchess Co., N. Y., and in Col. James Vanderburg's 5th Reg't, New York Militia. His name appears on the army pay-roll, dated Sept. 23, 1778, at which time he was only 16 years of age. Was a native of Rhode Island, and married Sarah Palmer in 1782, who was born in 1763. They moved to Chautauqua County in 1815 and settled on a farm in the town of Busti where they spent the remainder of their lives. She died Jan. 20, 1849, and is buried beside her husband. He is mentioned in the Pension List of 1840 as living in Busti with Ephraim Wilcox, a son. They had the following children: Eunice, Stephen, Jr., Ephraim, Able, Alfred, Lina, Roxanna.

WILLIAMS, DANIEL—Born at Norwich, Conn., Sept. 4, 1760. Died at Clymer, N. Y., February 13, 1846. Grave in Clymer Cemetery. He enlisted at Norwich, Mass., in April 1775, and served nine months as private in Capt. Abner Pomeroy's Company, Col. Fellow's Mass. Reg't. Enlisted in Sept., 1776, served fourteen months as private in Capt. Elijah Murray's and Capt. Chase's Companies, Col. Samuel Williams and Col. Pomeroy's Mass. Reg't, and was at the battle of Stillwater. Family records show that he was at the battle of Saratoga when Burgoyne surrendered, that he lost two fingers from one hand. He was the son of Elijah Williams and Lydia Longbottom who were married in 1756. Daniel Williams and family came to Chautauqua County in 1820 and settled in the town of Clymer, where he had been preceded by some of his sons. Young's History says he was the father of 16 children, 7 sons and 9 daughters, of whom four died in infancy. His wife, Lucretia, died July 31, 1834, aged 69 years. Her grave is beside husband in Clymer Cemetery.

WING, DANIEL—Born July 2, 1757, at Dartmouth, Mass. Date of death not ascertained. Grave in Clymer Cemetery. Enlisted Oct., 1780, served as private in Capt. Adiel Sherwood's Company, New York Militia. Was taken prisoner and confined one year at Montreal, was then moved to Prisoners' Island and kept until 1782, when he was exchanged and returned home. His brother, Benjamin, who enlisted with him was also taken prisoner at the same time. He applied for pension in 1832, while residing in Clymer, which was granted.

WOOD, CHARLES—Born June 27, 1760, at Falmouth, Novia Scotia. Died Feb. 4, 1844, at Harlinsburg, Mercer County, Pa. Enlisted in the American army at Mansfield, Conn., served under Capt. Shumway and Col. Huntington Connecticut Militia, from April, 1777, to Jan., 1778. In the latter year he served as Armorer at Lebanon, Pa., and in 1779 was Principal Field Armorer attached to 2nd Penna Brigade, discharged in May, 1780. Was at the battles of Sag Harbor, Long Island, Springfield. Applied for pension May, 1818, while a resident of Westport, N. Y. In 1821 he referred to his wife, Betsey, aged 54 years, and his son, Oscar, 16 years of age. In 1836 he was living in Jamestown, N. Y., where his son, Edward F., aged 46, also lived. He is mentioned in the Pension List of 1840 as living with Edward F. Wood in Jamestown. In 1843, he was living with a son at Mercer County, Pa. His wife died in Jamestown Feb. 6, 1840.

YOUNG, SAMUEL—Born in 1762 at Middletown, Conn. Died July 17, 1848. Grave in Dewittville Cemetery, town of Chautauqua. No record of his service in the Revolutionary war. Married Elizabeth Hubbard Brainard, at Old Haddam, Conn., in 1786. Moved to Vermont in 1793 and to Chautauqua County, N. Y., in 1816, settling on lot 54 in the town of Ellery. They had four sons, Samuel, Jr., David, Zenas and Enoch, and a daughter, Phoebe Hubbard. He was locally known as a Revolutionary soldier.

Benjamin Bosworth Chapter, D.A.R.
Silver Creek, N. Y.

Regent: ALICE KENT CHRISTY
Historical Committee: ALICE KENT CHRISTY
HARRIET WARD THOMAS
PHILENA MEAD WILLIAMS

Soldiers of the American Revolution who at one time resided in, or whose graves are located in one of the towns of Arkwright, Hanover, Sheridan, Villenova, Chautauqua County, N. Y.

ALLEN, MOSES—Born Sept., 1742. Died March 5, 1831, at Sheridan, Chautauqua County, N. Y. Grave in West Sheridan Cemetery. He enlisted while living in New Haven, Conn., and served in Captain Morris Company and Colonel Philiph B. Bradley's Regiment of Short Servys. Married Achsa, who was born September, 1742, and died March 4, 1834.

BALL, MATHIAS—Date of birth not ascertained. Died in 1839 in Villenova, Chautauqua County, N. Y. Grave in Villenova Cemetery. Native of Germany, came to America prior to the Revolution, settled in Schoharie County, N. Y. Said to have been a Revolutionary soldier.

BARNES, REUBEN—Born April 22, 1756, at North Harem, New Haven County, Conn. Died at Forestville, Chautauqua County, N. Y. Grave in Forestville Cemetery, Town of Hanover. Enlisted April 10 or 12, at Litchfield, Conn. Served seven months as private in Capt. Porter's Company under Col. Wooster. Re-enlisted under Eli Smith. Residence at time of application for pension, October 12, 1832, Winfield, Herkimer County, N. Y. Lived with Dennis Barnes at time of his death. On Pension List of 1840. In Arkwright on April 18, 1838, Mrs. Barnes, wife of Reuben Barnes, died, aged 67 years.

BUSH, STEPHEN—Born 1759. Died May 16, 1842. Buried in Sheridan Cemetery. He served in Mass. and Conn. troops in the War of the Revolution. At date of payment of pension he had been a resident of Sheridan, N. Y., for 33 years and previous thereto he resided at Munson, Hampshire County, Mass. His wife, Ziefiha, died Oct. 2, 1813, age 54 years. The first meeting of the Methodist Society of Sheridan was held at his home in 1809. He is mentioned in Pension List of 1840, residing with Stephen Bush, Jr., in Sheridan.

CLARK, Lieut. ELIAS—Born July 30, 1755. Died Aug. 3, 1845, at Villenova, Chautauqua County, N. Y. Grave in Hamlet Cemetery. He served as private in regiment commanded by Col. Levingston. He served as First Lieutenant during part of war. At the time of his application for pension in 1831 he had been a resident of Villenova for ten years and previous thereto had resided at Veteran, Tioga County, N. Y. He left children Josiah, Peter, James, Elizabeth, wife of John Frost, and Margaret, wife of Jessie Jay, and Samuel. He is men-

43

tioned in the Pension List of 1840 as residing with Jessie Jay.

COOLEY, ABNER—Born in 1751 in Palmer, Mass. Died in 1832 at Forestville, Chautauqua County, N. Y. He enlisted at Palmer, Mass., in 1775, as private under Capt. Silvanus Walker and Col. Timothy Danielson. He married Marie Chapin.

CRANSTON, SAMUEL—Born April 12, 1752, at Newport, Rhode Island. Died April 19, 1830, at Sheridan, Chautauqua County, N. Y. Grave in Sheridan Cemetery. He enlisted while living at Scituate, Rhode Island, in Sept., 1776, and served as a private and sergeant at various times, two years in all, under Capt. James Williams, Stephen Sheldon, William Howard, Simeon Harrindan, Samuel Wilbur and Jonathan Knight and Cols. Cooke and Barton. Was in Sullivan's Expedition to Rhode Island. He married Zilpha King, Nov. 23, 1780, at Scituate, R. I. In 1840, she was 80 years of age and living with her son, William, in the town of Hanover. She died June 15, 1844. They had children, Sarah, John, Freelove, Esther, Samuel, Peleg, Zilpha, Naoma, Barzillia, Hannah, Abraham, Serena, Helen Lindsay, and William.

CLOTHIER, JESSE—Born in 1760. Died in 1850. Grave in Doty Cemetery. Town of Hanover, Chautauqua County, N. Y. He served as a private for various lengths of time from 1776 to 1777 under Capt. Root, Col. Smith, Capt. Smith, Lieut. Israel Thomas and Capt. Wm. Douglas. He enlisted at Hancock, Berkshire County, Mass. Residence at date of application for pension, Gerard Township, Erie County, Pa. He was engaged in the Battle of Bennington. In Pension List of 1840 living with A. R. Clothier in town of Sheridan.

DARLING, JOHN—Born 1757, in Germany. Died Feb. 24, 1854, near Silver Creek, Chautauqua County, age 97 years. He enlisted at Poughkeepsie, N. Y., in 1776. He served as private in Capt. Fundy's Company under Col. Livingston, New York Militia. He also belonged to the Cooper Rangers of Dutchess County, N. Y. He was in the Battle of White Plains, and at the Surrender of Burgoyne. He married Rebecca Dalrymple, Jan. 8, 1815, at Hanover, N. Y. Grave marked with Goverment headstone and D. A. R. bronze marker.

ENSIGN, OTIS—Born Feb. 18, 1762, at Hartford, Conn. Died Oct. 4, 1855, at Sheridan, Chautauqua County, N. Y. Buried in Sheridan Center Cemetery. His father, Elephalet Ensign, was killed by Indians in Wyoming Massacre, 1778. Otis enlisted at the age of 16 years and was denounced by his uncle who was a strong Tory, because he enlisted in patriot forces. He served five years in all under Capts. Mills, Strong, Gideon, and Flowers and Cols. Philps, Swift and Austin. Was with Washington at the crossing of Delaware and at Valley Forge and was one of the guards over Major Andre at the time he was hung; came to Sheridan, built the first frame barn in that town, attended first Town Meeting and served for several years on the Town Board. He married Mary Patrick, 1st, and Hannah Dickenson, 2nd. Mary was the mother of his children, Elizabeth, William, Seth, Otis, Thomas, John, Seymour, and others. Was on 1840 Pension List. His wife, Mary died Jan. 8, 1842, aged 73 years.

FERRY, JOHN—Born July 9, 1754. Died July 16, 1832, at Forestville, Chautauqua County, N. Y. Grave in Pioneer Cemetery, Town of Hanover. He served as private in New York Line, First Reg't,

BENJAMIN BOSWORTH CHAPTER, SILVER CREEK, N. Y.

Col. Goose VanSchaick, N. Y., in the Revolution, page 32. He married Susannah Mum, Dec. 8, 1772. She served part of the time as nurse while he was in service; to them were born eight children.

FERRY, SUSANNAH—Born Dec. 17, 1752. Died 1830. She was the wife of John Ferry, married Dec. 8, 1772. Served all or part of the time as nurse while her husband was in service. Grave in Pioneer Cemetery, Town of Hanover.

FRINK, THOMAS—Born March 3, 1762. Died June 9, 1852. Grave supposed to be in Nashville, town of Hanover. Enlisted in Mass. Militia, Feb. 17, 1777, serving until Feb. 17, 1780, under Capt. Alexander, Capt. Daniel Pilsbury, Col. Negglesworth, Col. Smith. Was in battle of Rhode Island and Brandywine. Applied for pension which was granted, while residing at Madison County, N. Y. Became a resident of town of Hanover, Chautauqua County, N. Y., in 1823. He held the rank of Fifer in the army. His wife's name was Sylvia Pendleton. She was born in 1763 and died in 1851. His sons were: John, Alonzo, Loren, Sylvester, Thomas and Harvey. They were married in South Hadley, Mass. He is mentioned in the Pension List of 1840 as residing with his son, Harvey, in the town of Hanover.

GAGE, ASA—Born July 22, 1756, in England. Came to America with his two brothers. Died Jan. 26, 1837, in Hanover. Chautauqua County, N. Y. Grave in Smith's Mills Cemetery, town of Hanover. He was a "Minute Man" and marched in the alarm, April 19, 1775. Served seven years in War of Revolution in Mass. Militia and Mass. Regiment of Guards. He was in the Battle of Trenton, Christmas night, 1777. He married Mary Boton, who was born Feb. 22, 1761, and died Jan. 3, 1859. They were the parents of thirteen children, eleven of whom were living in 1840. Grave marked with D. A. R. bronze marker.

GREGORY, ESBON—Born about 1757. Date of death and location of grave not known. Was a resident of the town of Hanover, Chautauqua County, N. Y. Was Revolutionary soldier, serving as private in Massachusetts Militia, and is mentioned in the Pension List of 1830, aged 73, and residing in Chautauqua County, N. Y.

HATCH, NATHAN—Born 1757. Died about 1847. Went to Wisconsin in 1843 and died there. Enlisted 1776, serving in company of Capt. Hodges, and in New York Militia. Was granted pension and his name appears on the Pension Lists of 1830 and 1840. Became a resident of the town of Carroll in 1829, and in 1840 was residing with Edmund Hatch in the town of Arkwright.

HOLMES, ORSAMUS—Born Oct. 11, 1757, at Pembroke, Mass. Died Aug. 26, 1835 at the home of his son, Abner, at Killbuck, Ohio. Grave in Cemetery at Killbuck, Ohio. Enlisted at Pittsfield, Mass., in May, 1775, under Capt. William Lusk, Col. Eaton, joining Gen. Montgomery's army at Crown Point. Enlisted in Dec., 1775, was with the army before Quebec. Enlisted in April, 1776, and proceeded with the army to Ticonderoga and Mt. Independence, attached to Gen. Patterson's brigade. Re-enlisted in Dec. 1776, in a company of Rangers attached to a Green Mountain corps and participated in the capture of Mt. Defiance. A little later venturing outside the lines he was taken prisoner and confined on board a prison ship at Quebec. Here he remained a prisoner for several months, making one unsuccessful attempt to escape. A month later another desperate and successful attempt to break away from his prison was made by Mr. Holmes and two companions. After many days of severe hardship and privation, traveling through dense forests and swollen streams, they reached the frontier settlement of Monkton, Vt., on the fourteenth day of their escape. This closed his service as a soldier. On the 18th day of Feb., 1780 he married Ruth Webb at Charlestown, N. H. In 1805 he purchased a farm from the Holland Land Company in the town of Sheridan, Chautauqua County, N. Y., taking possession of it with his family in June that year. Here he remained a prominent and influential citizen for many years. Mr. and Mrs. Holmes had eleven children: Alanson, who married Olive Lee, and died in 1818; Abner, who married Betsey Young, and died in 1859; Brilliant, who married John Scott, and died in 1853; Origen, who died in 1806, aged 18; Ruth, who married Dr. John E. Marshall; Augustine, who died in 1802, aged 9 years; Myron, who married Sally Taylor; Asher, who married Eliza Ellmore, and died in 1854; Laurana, married Louis Wooster, and and died in 1860; William, died in infancy; Augustine 2nd, who married Sarah Lee, and died in 1849. Mr. Holmes was awarded a pension and is mentioned in the Pension List of 1830. Following his death in Aug., 1835, his wife, Ruth, passed away, Oct. 7, of the same year. Her grave is beside husband at Killbuck, Ohio.

HAMLIN, ZACCHIAS—Born at Sharon, Conn., about 1757. Died previous to 1836 while a resident of the town of Hanover, Chautauqua County, N. Y. While a resident of Columbia County, N. Y., he enlisted in the winter of 1776, serving nine months in Capt. Roderick Beebe's Company, N. Y. troops. In 1778, served three months in Capt. Chapman's Company, Col. Van Alstyne's Reg't. Was also out on alarm service for three months. Was granted a pension in 1833 while a resident of Villenova, Chautauqua County, N. Y.

HERRICK, EPHRIAM—Born 1755. Died Feb. 10, 1842 at Sheridan, Chautauqua County, N. Y. Buried in West Sheridan Cemetery. He served in the Mass. troops and in the U. S. Navy during the War of the Revolution. Certificate No. 6892. Albany, N. Y., Agency. Mentioned on Pension List of 1840. He left no widow, but one child, Alfred Herrick.

INGRAHAM, WILLIAM—Date of birth and death not ascertained. Grave, Evergreen Cemetery, Hanover Center, Chautauqua County, N. Y. Service, Rank, Continental, enlisted in Woodbury Conn., for duration of war in Capt. Ferrand's Company, Col. Mosley's Reg't of Connecticut Line, 4th Continental Brigade.

INGRAHAM, AMOS—Born about 1755. Died Aug. 11, 1839. Grave in Hanover Center Cemetery, town of Hanover, Chautauqua County, N. Y. Enlisted at New London, Conn., in April, 1777, serving one year as private in Capt. Ebenezer Lathrop's and Lee Lay's Company, Conn. Militia. Was granted pension in 1823. He became a resident of the town of Hanover in 1809. His wife, Sarah, died Dec. 24, 1836, in her 81st year. Her grave is in family lot in Hanover Cemetery.

BENJAMIN BOSWORTH CHAPTER, SILVER CREEK, N. Y.

JOHNSON, JOHN—Born 1756 at Hempstead, Long Island, N. Y. Died June 26, 1838, at Silver Creek, Chautauqua County, N. Y. Grave in Glenwood Cemetery, town of Hanover. He served as a private in Revolutionary war, N. Y. troops. He married Elizabeth Peck, who was born about 1759, and died Feb. 9, 1840. Recorded in Pension Office, Book "E," Vol. 4, Page 22. On Pension List of 1831.

KENT, JOHN—Born in Vermont in 1753. Died in 1834 in the town of Villenova, Chautauqua County, N. Y. Grave supposed to be in that town. He was a soldier in the American Revolution, attained the rank of Sergeant in Vermont Militia. He is mentioned in the Pension List of 1831. He settled in the town of Villenova in 1809 and built the first saw-mill and grist-mill in the south-east part of that town. He married Mary Whipple. His son, John, became a Methodist minister, removing to Livingston County, N. Y.; James removed to Ohio; Polly married Dr. Dighton and after his death a Mr. Moffitt.

KIRKLAND, WILLIAM—Born 1759 on the Atlantic Ocean of Scotch parentage. Died May 10, 1830, at Balltown, town of Hanover, Chautauqua County, N. Y. Grave in Balltown Cemetery, town of Hanover. He served as a private in New York Line, First Regiment. Tombstone marked: "A Soldier of the Revolution." He married Margaret Stone, who died Jan. 10, 1835.

LOVE, ROBERT—Born Feb. 2, 1757, at Coventry, Rhode Island. Died Feb. 20, 1846, at Forestville, Chautauqua County, N.Y. Grave in Pioneer Cemetery, town of Hanover. He served as private and teamster for various lengths of time in different Massachusetts regiments and State troops; he was in the seige of Boston, Battle of White Plains, Capture of Burgoyne, White Marsh and Oriskany. He was also in the War of 1812, and served in the Company of his second son, Capt. Levi Love of Madison County, N. Y. He was the oldest son of Thomas Love and grandson of Gabriel Love, emigrants from Sutrim, Ireland, of Scotch-Irish family. He married first Mary Cutting at Athol, Mass., May 27, 1778, who died Nov. 29, 1790, leaving three sons and three daughters. Married, second time, Dolly Tompkins of New Paltz, N. Y., 1794, by whom he had two sons and one daughter.

MATHER, JOSEPH—Born Jan. 28, 1756, at Lyme, Connecticut. Died March 21, 1848. Grave supposed to be in Cemetery in Villenova. He enlisted at Lyme, Conn., in 1776, served seven months as private in Capt. Samuel Mather's Company, Col. Erastus Wolcott's Connecticut Reg't. Enlisted in Jan., 1777, in Capt. Palmer's Company, was under Colonels Harris, Ely and Arnold, and was in Gen. Spencer's Rhode Island Expedition, serving one year. Enlisted in 1778, served one month and a half as private in Capt. Holmes' Company, was in Gen. Sullivan's Expedition, was in the Battle of Rhode Island. In 1779 he enlisted on board the ship "Trumbull" under Captains Saltonstall and Hinman, serving three months. Was granted pension in 1832 while living in Chenango County, N. Y., and his name appears in the Pension List of 1840 as residing with John Mather in the town of Villenova, Chautauqua County, N. Y., aged 85 years. He married in 1780 and had children, no names stated.

McMANUS, CHRISTOPHER—Born Aug. 12, 1758. Died June 14, 1849. Grave in Cemetery at Forestville, Chautauqua County, N. Y. He was a soldier in the Revolution, attaining the rank of Sergeant in New Jersey Militia. He is mentioned in the Pension Lists of 1819 and 1840. He became a resident of Hanover in 1816.

NASH, SILAS—Born June 14, 1762, at Norwalk, Fairfield County, Conn. Died Jan. 6, 1852, at Hanover, Chautauqua County, N. Y., age 90 years. Grave in Nashville Cemetery, town of Hanover. He served as a private in N. Y. troops for various lengths of time from May 1, 1779 to 1782. He was engaged in the battles of Ridgefield, Fairfield, Norwalk, and Green Farms. He married Hannah Peacock of Perrysburg, N. Y., July 14, 1844. He received a pension, and is on list of 1830 and 1840. His widow, Hannah, was united in marriage to James Fyrer, Sept. 21, 1862. Grave marked with Government head stone and bronze D. A. R. marker.

NAUGHTON, SOLOMON—Born in May, 1750 or 1751, at Farmington, Conn. Died in 1844 at Villenova, Chautauqua County, N. Y. While residing at New Cannan he enlisted in the summer of 1776 for one month, with New York troops, under Capt. Bostwick, Col. Whiting's Reg't. Re-enlisted in fall of 1776, serving four months in Capt. Bostwick's Company, Col. Whiting's Reg't, and in May, 1777, in the same company and regiment commenced another service of four weeks and again of five months. Was allowed a pension in 1832 while residing at Shoreham, Vt. In 1837 he was living in Chautauqua County, N. Y., and is mentioned in the Pension List of 1840 as residing with G. B. Aldrich in the town of Villenova.

NEVINS, THOMAS—Born May 25, 1748, at Hollis, New Hampshire. Died in year 1814 at Hanover, Chautauqua County, N. Y. Grave in Hanover. Enlisted July, 1775, under Capt. Thornton as recorded in New Hampshire State Papers on Hammond, Vol. 17, Revolutionary Rolls, Vol. 4. He married Rebecca Willoughby about 1770. She was born in 1749 and died in 1837. In 1808 moved with their four sons and three daughters from Hanover, New Hampshire, to town of Hanover, Chautauqua County, N. Y. Children: Hannah, Susannah, Rebecca, Jeriah, Bridget, Anna, Thomas, Henry, Sam, Nathan.

OLMSTEAD, JAMES—Born April 5, 1755, at Norwalk, Conn. Died Jan. 4, 1841, Arkwright, Chautauqua County, N. Y. Grave in Arkwright. Enlisted at Norwalk, Conn., as private under Capt. Beach and Col. Herman Swift; later, summer of 1777, as a "Minute Man" under Capt. Gregory and Col. Swift. Was present at the burning of Fairfield and Norwalk. Married in Connecticut.

OSBORNE, DANIEL—Born Dec. 30, 1751. Died Oct. 10, 1845, at Villenova, Chautauqua County, N. Y. Enlisted at Newburg, N. Y., in 1776, serving three years as private in Company of Capt. Philip Debois Bavier, Col. Lewis Debois' 5th Reg't, N. Y. Line. Was in the Battle of Fort Montgomery in the Command of Gen. James Clinton. Was allowed pension in 1818 and is mentioned in the Pension List of 1840, aged 89, residing in Cherry Creek, Chautauqua County, N. Y.

PHELPS, CORNELIUS—Born about 1763. Died in March, 1844, at Evans, Erie County, N. Y. Location of grave not ascertained. He is mentioned in the

BENJAMIN BOSWORTH CHAPTER, SILVER CREEK, N. Y.

Pension List of 1840 as residing in the town of Hanover, Chautauqua County, N. Y. He enlisted at Linn, Conn., in the spring of 1781, in the company of Capt. Bissell and Capt. Douglass, and served until the end of the war. His wife, Philena, in 1855, was residing in Cattaraugus County, N. Y., applied for Bounty Land.

PRATT, STEPHEN—Born in 1753. Date of death and location of grave not ascertained. He was a soldier in the Revolution, attaining the rank of Corporal and Sergeant in Massachusetts Militia. Was granted a pension in 1831 while residing in Chautauqua County, N. Y., and is also mentioned in the Pension List of 1840 as residing in the town of Arkwright.

PHILLIPS, THOMAS—Born Sept. 1, 1762. Died May 14, 1848, in Villenova, Chautauqua County, N. Y. Grave in Villenova Cemetery. He resided in Villenova for thirteen years before applying for a pension and previous thereto at Brookfield, Madison County, N. Y. After his death, the pension went to his widow, Sally, who died Jan. 15, 1859. She left the following children, Sarah D. Phillips, John Clark, James Clark, Luther Clark, and Welcome Clark, children of a former marriage. He served in Mass. troops. On Pension List of 1840.

RATHBUN, SOLOMON—Born March 3, 1764. Died Aug. 29, 1849. Grave in Rathbun Cemetery, town of Hanover, Chautauqua County, N. Y. He entered Colonial service at the age of fifteen and served as a private for three years in the Revolutionary army. He belonged to the Vermont Rangers, served under Captains Moody and Dustin, and at one time enlisted in the First New Hampshire Regiment. He was engaged in the battles of Morrisania, New Rochelle, and King Street. Resided at Truxton, Cortland Co., N. Y., at time of application for pension. On Pension List of 1840. He married Eunice Fuller, Dec. 5, 1784. Eunice Fuller was born at Canajoharie, N. Y., Dec. 15, 1764, died March 12, 1806, at Forestville, N. Y. Children: Demarcus, Bulina, Titus, Elihue, Lucy, Almira Bulina, Mather.

SPENCER, REUBEN—Born 1752, in East Haddam, Conn. Died April 9, 1836, at Villenova, Chautauqua County, N. Y. Buried in Villenova. Was private in Connecticut Militia in the Revolution. Awarded pension in 1831. He had lived in Villenova, N. Y., for 15 years prior to application for pension and previous thereto at Litchfield, Conn. He left a widow, Mehitable, who died March 4, 1850, aged 88 years. Surviving her were three children, Halsey, Reuben, and John. Pension was granted wife after death of husband.

SPENCER, Rev. JOHN—Born 1758. Died in 1826 at Sheridan, Chautauqua County, N. Y. Buried in a part of ground contributed by him from his farm to the town of Sheridan for burial purposes. He served as a Lieutenant in Capt. Peter Van Rensselaer's Company, Col. Marinus Willet's Reg't, New York Levies, which was organized at Fort Herkimer, Oct. 7, 1781. He conducted the first religious meeting held in the town in 1807.

SCHOFIELD, ENOS—Born Jan. 26, 1758, at Stamford, Conn. Died Dec. 15, 1836, at Nashville, town of Hanover, Chautauqua County, N. Y. Grave in Nashville Cemetery. Enlisted in the spring of 1776, serving as private in Capt Gilbert's Company, Col. Mead's Reg't

New York troops, for seven and one-half months. Enlisted in May, 1777, served six months in Capt. Porter's Company, Conn. troops. Was granted pension and is mentioned in the Pension List of 1830 as residing in Chautauqua County. He was a weaver by trade. He married Hannah Schofield in 1779. They had three children, Clarissa, Betsey and Arunah.

SPINK, SHIBNAH—Born Aug. 1, 1757, in East Greenwich, R. I. Died 1846, in Hanover, Chautauqua County, N. Y. Grave in Doty Cemetery, town of Hanover. He served as a private through a large part of Revolutionary War. He was engaged in the struggle known as the Battle of Long Island and passed through the winter encampment at Valley Forge, 1777-78. He was one of the few Quakers who took up arms for their country. He married Delight Clothier in Berkshire County, Mass. She was a daughter of John Clothier, a Revolutionary soldier. One son, Norman Spink, was a soldier in War of 1812, another son, Hon. Cyrus Spink, was a member elect to Congress at time of death.

THATCHER, ELIAKIM — Born March 30, 1763, at Lebanon, Conn. Died Jan. 14, 1848, at Arkwright, Chautauqua County, N. Y. Grave in a pasture on farm of Ransom Mathewson, near Burnham Hollow. Service rendered, one year as teamster under Captains Lamband, Nigley, and Colonels Hay and Hughes. Pension papers credit him with one year's service in quartermaster's department. Children: Chester, Charles, Orestres. On 1840 Pension List.

THOMPSON, NATHAN—Born June 5, 1764, Gloucester, Rhode Island. Died Feb. 24, 1839, Sheridan, Chautauqua County, N. Y. Buried in Sheridan Cemetery. While a resident of Charlton, Worcester County, Mass., he enlisted in March, 1781, as a private in Capt. Chamber's Company, Col. Smith's Mass. Reg't; transferred to Capt. Main's Company, Col. Sprout's Mass. Regiment; transferred to Capt. Haskell's Company, Col. Henry Jackson's Regiment and was discharged June 30, 1784. He moved to Sheridan in 1828 and purchased the farm from the Holland Land Company on which he died. He was married in Cheshire, Mass. On Pension List of 1831.

VAN CAMP, ISAAC—Born June, 1759, in Waring, Ulster County, N. Y. Died in Forestville, April 20, 1843. Grave in Forestville Cemetery, town of Hanover. Enlisted at Canajoharie, N. Y., for ten months, served as private under Capt. Van Ness and Lansing. Re-enlisted 1777 for nine months under Capt. Simonds and Colonels Hale and Schuyler. Re-enlisted 1779 for four months as 2nd Sergeant. Enlisted later under Capt. Diffendorf and Col. Clyde. Resided at Barre, Orleans County, N. Y., in 1832, at which time he applied for pension and it was allowed.

WARNER, NATHANIEL—Born July 4, 1767, at East Haddam, Conn. Died July 28, 1843, at Cambridge, N. Y. Grave in Hamlet Cemetery, Villenova, Chautauqua County, N. Y. He enlisted in 1781 and served as private in Capt. Richards' Company, Col. Sherman's and Col. Swifts Conn. Reg'ts. Was discharged in 1783. Was awarded pension and is mentioned in the Pension List of 1840. Was married July 4, 1790, to Lucinda Avery. They moved from Herkimer County, N. Y., to Villenova in 1820. Their children were: Reuben, who died at the age of 21; Judah, Obadiah, Dema, Nathaniel, Jr., Jeremiah, Abigail, Lucinda, Reuben.

BENJAMIN BOSWORTH CHAPTER, SILVER CREEK, N. Y.

WHITE, JAMES—Born 1758. Died April 26, 1843. Buried in Sheridan Cemetery, Sheridan, Chautauqua County, N. Y. He served as private with Massachusetts troops, War of Revolution. Last payment of pension was made April 10, 1843, for the period from Sept. 4, 1842, to March 4, 1843. On Pension Lists of 1830 and 1840. At the date of payment the pensioner had been a resident of Sheridan, N. Y., for thirty-three years and previous thereto had resided at Madison, Madison County, N. Y.

WOOD, WILLIAM—Born at Westborough, Mass., 1764. Died Feb. 12, 1850, at home at Arkwright, Chautauqua County, N. Y. Grave in Christian Meeting House Grounds, Burnham's Hollow, N. Y. Served as private and later as Sergeant in Mass. regiments, from Feb. 22, 1781, to January 4, 1783. His father was Revolutionary soldier, same name. Pension application, April 7, 1818, at Springfield, Vt., and is mentioned in the 1840 Pension List as residing at Arkwright with Arna Wood. His wife was Sally Andrews. She died at Dewittville, Nov. 30, 1844. The following children survived him: Arna, Elmer, Cyrus, Anna, Philips, Lucretia, Emery, Lois Scott, Luceba, Eli, Elyah, and three grandchildren: Hiram, Harvey and Palmeo Denison.

Patterson Chapter, D. A. R.
Westfield, N. Y.

Regent: CATHERINE PATTERSON CRANDALL
Historical Committee: ALTA OWEN FLAGLER
JULIA M. STONE
ANNA BROCKWAY McGINNIES
MARGARET D. FOX

Soldiers of the American Revolution who at one time resided in, or whose graves are located in one of the towns of: Mina, Ripley, Sherman, Westfield, West Portland, and part of the town of Chautauqua, Chautauqua County, N. Y.

ADAMS, LEVI—Born Feb. 17, 1754, in Dutchess County, N. Y. Died Dec. 26, 1833. Grave probably in one of the cemeteries in the town of Ripley, Chautauqua County, N. Y. Enlisted Sept. 12, 1776, at Windham County, Conn., for two months under Capt. Sherebiah Butler, Conn. Militia; was in the Battle of White Plains. Enlisted again, same year, under Capt. Sanford Kingsbury Col. McLaren's Reg't. Enlisted in July 1777 under Capt. Parkins and early in the summer of 1778 under Capt. Ziba Hunt, 2 weeks service in the protection of New London, Conn. troops. Enlisted March 1, 1780, at Pawlet, Vt., where he had removed a few days before, serving under Capt. John Stark, to pursue Indians, who had committed depredations. Enlisted again in Aug. or Sept., 1781, under Capt. Samuel Willard, also in 1782. Removed from Pawlet, Vt., in 1794, to Otsego County, N. Y., and in 1826 to Ripley, Chautauqua County, N. Y. Was granted a pension in 1832, while a resident of Ripley.

ANDERSON, SAMUEL—Born 1762. Died June 27, 1837. Grave in Union Cemetery, towns of Westfield and Portland. He enlisted in Cherry Valley, New York, in 1777, served as private in Capt. Robert McKean and Benjamin Hick's Companies, Col. Van Schaick's New York Reg't. He enlisted for the war and his name last appeared on the muster roll for April, 1783, and was discharged at the close of the war. He was in the battle of Monmouth and the Siege of Yorktown. Was allowed a pension on his application executed May 1, 1818, while living in Portland, Chautauqua County, N. Y. In 1820 he referred to his wife, Jerusha, and to his daughters, Sally, aged 25 years, and Betsey, aged 18 years, son Samuel, aged 20 years, and grand-son Allen Shepard Sisson, aged 3 years and 3 months, whose mother was dead and father living in Indiana. The wife of Samuel Anderson died July 18, 1837, aged 75 years. Her grave is beside husband. Other children: Polly, Jane, Nancy, Sophia.

BARNS, CALVIN—Born about 1766. Date of death and location of grave not ascertained. Young's History says he was a pioneer settler of the town of Portland, Chautauqua County, was a soldier of the Revolution and of the War of 1812. Was wounded in the battle of Buffalo in December, 1813. He is mentioned in the

Pension List of 1840 as residing in Portland. He was the first postmaster of Portland—the office was created in 1818 and was located on his farm, 6 miles east of the village of Westfield. His wife, Rachel, died Sept. 28, 1853, aged 82 years.

BARNHART, PETER—Born March 31, 1751. Died Aug. 13, 1836, aged 85 years. Grave in Mayville Cemetery. Was native of Germany, came to this country with his brother when about 16 years of age. They lived in Baltimore for a time and later went to Pennsylvania. Peter enlisted in the Lancaster County Militia. Was private in Capt. Philip Buck's Company, 3rd Battalion, Elizabeth Township, Lancaster County. See page 325, Vol. vii, Penn. Archives, 5th Series. He emigrated to Chautauqua County in 1805 and settled on lot 18 in the town of Chautauqua. His sons, Jonathan, Peter and Henry also settled in the town of Chautauqua. Molly, wife of Peter Barnhart, died Jan. 15, 1835, aged 82 years. They had 11 children. Her grave is beside her husband.

BURNHAM, DANIEL—Born in 1762. Died Sept. 10, 1844, while residing in the town of Portland, Chautauqua County, N. Y. Enlisted in April, 1779, served under Capt. John St. John, Col. Philip Burr Bradley, General Huntington's Brigade, Connecticut Line. Later transferred to Capt. Samuel Hoyt's Company, serving to Feb. 6, 1780. Was united in marriage to Hannah Burr, Feb. 20, 1816, at Leicester, N. H. Applied for pension in 1818 and in 1831 applied for restoration to pension rolls, having been granted pension and then dropped under the property act of 1820. In his application for restoration he gave schedule of property amounting to something like $1,000 in value, and "his dependent family, self 69 years, wife 58 years, stepdaughter, Mycercia Newell, 22, Benjamin Burnham Newell 6, Joseph Newell 4, and a hired-man. Mrs. Newell did the housework, and spinning, receiving maintenance for self and children, her husband being dead or in parts unknown. In 1835, he was residing in Portland, Chautauqua County, and he is mentioned in the Pension List of 1840. His wife, Hannah, applied for pension in 1853, at which time she was 83 years of age, and residing in Portland. In 1855 she was residing in Decatur, Mich.

BELL, ARTHUR—Born at Paxton, Pa., Jan. 12, 1752. Died Aug. 6, 1834. Grave in Lower Ripley Cemetery with D. A. R. marker: "Bird's Pa. Mill. Rev. War." Served three years in the American army during the Revolution and in 1802 or 1803, accompanied by his son, William, moved to Western New York, locating in the town of Westfield. They were prominent in the formation of the First Presbyterian Church at the "Cross-Roads" in 1817. His wife, Eleanor Montgomery, was born Sept. 2, 1768, and died Dec. 2, 1839.

BENSON, JOEL—Was born in 1749. Died at Ripley, Chautauqua County, N. Y., in 1837. Served with New York troops as private and as an artificer and guide to scouting parties from 1778 to the close of the war. Was three times wounded. Was granted a pension and is mentioned in the Pension List of 1831, aged 82, and residing in Chautauqua County. He married Mary Shaw, and their daughter, Alice, married William Mann.

BENNETT, BENJAMIN—Born Feb. 13, 1756. Died Sept. 12, 1841. Grave in Lower Ripley Cemetery with D. A. R.

marker. He enlisted in the American army July 6, 1775, served five months as private in Capt. Joseph Height's Company, Col. Charles Webb's Connecticut Reg't. Enlisted Nov. 24, 1776, served as private and Sergeant until June 7, 1783, in Captains Eli Leavenworth's and Lemuel Clift's Companies, Col. William Douglass', David Deming's, Return J. Meighs' and Zebulon Butler's Connecticut Regiments. Was granted pension on his application March 24, 1818, while a resident of Milton, Saratoga County, N. Y. He married Oct. 9, 1784, Sarah St. John. She died June 9, 1787. He married Sept. 9, 1790, at Milton, N. Y., Eunice Ferre, widow of William Johnson. She was born July 27, 1756, and died Aug. 8, 1843, at Ripley. Their children were: Sally, born 1791, died 1813; a child, name not on record, born 1793; Azariah, 1st, born 1795, died July 20, 1796; Lyman, born 1797; Azariah, 2nd, born May, 1800; Zadock and Benjamin, dates of birth not on record. The grave of Eunice, his wife, is beside husband in Ripley Cemetery, unmarked.

BIRD, NAHANIEL—Born in Salisbury, Conn., May 17, 1763. Died Jan. 12, 1847, in the 80th year of his age. Grave in Westfield Cemetery. At the age of sixteen he enlisted in the American army for three months and after that for the duration of the war. Enlisted at Tyringham, Mass., served as private in Captain Christopher Woodridge's Company, Col. John Graeton's Reg't until Dec. 30, 1783. Was wounded in the leg, and after his discharge, it is recorded, he begged his way home, barefoot, and almost naked. Was married at New Marlborough, Mass., to Hannah Bullard, November 8, 1787. Lived in New Marlborough until about 1812 and in 1815 moved to Chautauqua County and took up lands near Jamestown. His eldest son, Capt. Amos Bird, a soldier of the war of 1812, settled there, while the father settled in Westfield. During his active and prominent life in Chautauqua County he was known as Colonel Nathaniel Bird, the title being attained it is supposed by his connection with some of the early military organizations. He was one of the trustees of the First Presbyterian Church of Westfield and in 1820 contracted to carry mail, on horseback, once a week from Erie to Buffalo. He also inaugurated the stage routes for mail, and in 1824, in company with his son, Ira Bird, established a daily stage post, chaises being used on portion of the route. He erected the toll-bridges over "18 mile" and Cattaraugus Creeks. Was granted a pension in 1818. Up to the year 1800 there seems to have been only sons in his family but later Mary, Julia, and Belinda are mentioned. The children mentioned in his pension application were the younger ones, Frederick, aged 18; Ira, 16; Emily, 13; Caroline, 11; Lorenzo, 6; and Charles L., 4. Until recently, a grand-daughter, Camilla Foster, wife of Dr. Orson Hoyt, was living in Buffalo. Col. Bird and his wife died in the same year, 1847, having lived nearly sixty years together. Their graves, with those of several of their children, are in the Westfield Cemetery, and the name of Nathaniel Bird is among those on the monument at the "Cross-Roads." He is mentioned in the Pension List of 1840.

BOND, BETHUEL—Was born May 20, 1763, at Dover, Dutchess County, N. Y. Died August 15, 1841, aged 78 years, 3 months and five days, grave in Mayville Cemetery. Residence at time of enlistment, Stockbridge, Mass. Date of enlistment, July 7, 1778, to Jan. 1, 1779. Served as private under Capt.

Enos Parker and Col. Jacob Garish, Mass. Militia. Enlisted July 18, 1779, to Aug. 22, 1779, served under Capt. Ambrose Hill and Col. Miles Powell. Enlisted July 21, 1780, to Oct. 27, 1780, served as Corporal under Capt. William Ford, Col. John Brown. Granted pension in 1832, while a resident of the town of Chautauqua. Is mentioned in the Pension List of 1840. Was united in marriage with Lydia Dolph, at Westfield, Washington County, N. Y., in 1791. She was born Jan. 9, 1774, and died August 9, 1845. Her grave is beside husband. She left eight surviving children: Laura, Olive, William D., Phebe, Ira, Bethuel, Jr., Gamaliel, Minor, Polly. The pension allowed mother was continued after her death to the children.

BRADLEY, LENT—Born in New Haven, Conn., 1751. Died Dec. 20, 1840, aged 89 years. Grave in Westfield Cemetery with D. A. R. marker: "Corp. Lent Bradley, Haven's Mass. Mil. Rev. War." Enlisted at Stockbridge, serving as private and later as Corporal; was a prisoner at Ticonderoga one winter. While in the Revolutionary army he was at one time out all night in a cold rain, suffering greatly from the exposure and was never able after to speak above a whisper. It is related of him that when his pension money came, he always gathered his grand-children about him and divided the money among them. He was in the fifth generation from William Bradley, ancestor, who was one of the first settlers of New Haven, Conn., and who brought with him armorial bearings given him by Richard II of England for services rendered the King. His first wife, Ann Bristol, was the mother of their children, Mary, William, John, Joel, Ann, and Cornelia. His second wife was Roxana Collins, of Ripley, who died May 17, 1854, aged 80 years, and whose grave is beside him in the Westfield Cemetery. He became a settler of Westfield in 1831, and is mentioned in the Pension List of 1840.

BRIGHAM, JONATHAN—Born Oct. 29, 1754, at Marlborough, Mass. Died July 26, 1848, aged 94 years. Grave in Mayville Cemetery, Mayville, N. Y. Was one of the "Minute Men" who responded to the call in April, 1775, under Capt. Daniel Burns and Col. Henshaw, Massachusetts Militia. Enlisted April, 1775, to Feb., 1776, serving as private in the Company of Capt. Barns and Col. Artemas Ward. Enlisted Oct. 2, 1777, as private under Capt. Morse and Col. Read. Residence at time of enlistment, Marlborough, Mass. Was at the battles of Bunker Hill and Saratoga. Applied for pension, April 30, 1818, at which time he was a resident of Chautauqua County. He moved from Oneida County, N. Y., in 1810, and settled in the town of Sheridan, Chautauqua County, and in 1813 moved to Mayville. His wife, Lydia, died Feb. 4, 1828, aged 70 years, and his wife, Lucy, May 3, 1842, aged 61 years. Both are buried beside him in the Mayville Cemetery. A son, Jonathan, Jr., born Oct. 13, 1791, died Sept. 3, 1819. A son, Samuel, died in 1811, and a son, John, died in 1828. Another son, Edward, born July 16, 1796, died December 16, 1876, aged 80 years, and is buried in the family lot at Mayville. Lucina Brigham died March 1, 1854, aged 54 years, 2 months. The name of Jonathan Brigham appears on the Pension List of 1840. His brother, John Brigham, who was also a soldier in the American Revolution, became a resident of Chautauqua County at an early part of the 19th century and his grave is in the Fredonia Cemetery.

CHASE, WILLIAM—Born Oct. 18, 1762. Is mentioned in the Pension List of 1840 as residing at Westfield, Chautauqua County, N. Y. In Sept., 1844, he asked transfer to Vermont where he had gone to reside with daughter. Enlisted at Barre, Mass., May 6, 1782, for 3 years. Served under Capt. John Blanchard, 9th Mass. Reg't. Was assigned to Company at VerPlanchs Point, opposite West Point, and later his regiment was incorporated into one called the "American Regiment." Served 3 months in Militia at Barre, Mass., under Horatio Gates, Orderly Sergeant. While residing in Chautauqua County in 1832 he made application for pension which was granted. No record of his family has been obtained or date of his death.

COUCH, WILLIAM—Was born in Landisfield, Mass., 1759. Died at Westfield, N. Y., April 27, 1845, aged 86 years. Grave in Union Cemetery, with D. A. R. marker: "Wm. Couch, 12 Mass. Mil. Rev. War." Enlisted at the age of 17 years in Mass. Militia, his entire service embracing three enlistments. Was granted pension and is mentioned in the Pension List of 1840 as residing in Portland. He always carried a Bible and Psalm book in his knapsack, placed there by his mother, and when in camp the soldiers had daily worship. In later life he was active and prominent in the Presbyterian Church of Westfield. He came to Westfield in 1815. His wife, Abigail, died May 15, 1832, aged 66 years, and her grave is beside husband. Their sons, Hiram and Warren, who came with them to Westfield in 1815, also became active and prominent in the affairs of their community. They left many descendants.

DARROW, GEORGE—Born at Preston, Conn., March 31, 1764. Died Jan. 8, 1852, aged 87 years, 9 months and 8 days. Grave in Mayville Cemetery. Enlisted April 1, 1781, while living at New Concord, Columbia County, N. Y., served nine months as private in Capt. Marshall's Company, Col. Marinus Willett's New York Reg't, and also in Capt. George Darrow's, his father's Company, Col. McKinstry's N. Y. Reg't. Enlisted about the middle of March, 1782, as private in Capt. Whelp's Company, Col. G. Van Schaick's N. Y. Reg't. Discharged Dec. 16, 1782. Allowed a pension on his application, Oct. 19, 1829, while residing in Chautauqua County, N. Y. Referred to wife, name not stated, aged 60 years, in 1831. She died in 1841. In 1839 he was living in Knox County, Ohio, with son-in-law, Truman, or Freeman, Potter. In 1843, he was living in New York state with a son, probably Lafayette, whose grave is in another Cemetery near the Mayville Cemetery, where George Darrow is buried.

DICKSON, ROBERT—Born Feb. 10, 1763. Died Aug. 20, 1832. Grave in Cemetery, town of Ripley, Chautauqua County, N. Y. He was born in Cherry Valley, N. Y., and during the massacre at that settlement in 1778 his mother was killed. The terrible tragedy of her death so enraged the boy he tried to enlist in the Continental army to revenge the murder of his beloved mother, but being too young to enter the ranks as a soldier he was accepted as a drummer boy and served in that capacity until his age permitted entrance in the regular service. In 1809 he moved from Cherry Valley, N. Y., to Ripley, Chautauqua County, N. Y., where he purchased lands for his home. In 1815 he gave an acre of land in the settlement of Ripley for use as a buryingground and which is now the Cemetery where his grave is located with a D. A. R.

marker: "Robert Dickson, 7th N. Y. Mil. Rev. War." His wife, Olive, died Jan. 18, 1812, in the 48th year of her age, and her grave is beside husband. Their sons were Samuel, William, Robert C., Fayette and Andrew and their daughters were Jane, who married Joseph Cass, and Olive who married Judd W. Cass.

DUSTIN, MOSES—Born Jan. 26, 1765, on Merrimack River, about 40 miles from Boston, Mass. He is mentioned in the Pension List of 1840 as residing in the town of Ripley, Chautauqua County, N. Y. Resided at Londonderry, N. H., at the commencement of the Revolutionary War. Enlisted June, 1779, at Londonderry, N. H., as Fifer for three months in Company of Capt. Sinclair. In June or July, 1780, he served in a Company of Capt. Adkins, Col. Bartlett, and was at West Point when Arnold deserted. Applied for pension in 1832, which was granted. In 1851, in August, he removed to New Hampshire, at Stratford, where he had gone to live with one of his daughters. Another daughter lived in the same place. He was then a widower and his other children were scattered in different section of the country. A letter from Joshua Marshall, at Stratford, N. H., in Jan., 1851, states that Dutton is now quite deaf, blind with one eye and unable to see to read with the other.

DURAND, FISK—Born in Milford, Conn., in 1766. Died April 18, 1841, in the 75th year of his age. Grave in Westfield Cemetery with D. A. R. marker: "Musician Fisk Durand, Mead's Ct. Mil. Rev. War." Served for a time as a drummer boy in 1776 and in the spring of 1778 enlisted in Connecticut Militia in Company of Capt. Bradley and Col. Evans' Reg't. Marched to Horse-Neck where he remained until term expired. Enlisted in Sept. of 1779 for 7 or 8 months under Capt. Peter Perrit, Col. Mead, Henry Bull, Adjutant, Joseph Whitney, Serg't Major. Spent the winter at Horse-Neck and was discharged in the spring of 1780, whole time of service 30 months. Although young, he was in each term regularly enlisted, serving throughout each period as drummer, bound to strict military duty which he faithfully performed. His pay exceeded that of a private by 50 cents per month. He is mentioned in the Pension List of 1840. After the war he returned to his home in Milford where he remained until 1815 when he moved to Boulton, N. Y., later to the adjoining town of Kingsbury, and later in life came to Westfield, settling on what was known as the "Barney Farm" on the Sherman Road, where he remained until his death. His wife, Polly E., died April 13, 1839, in the 70th year of her age.

DYER, JONATHAN—Born April 8, 1764, at Newport, R. I. In 1840 he was living in Westfield, Chautauqua County, N. Y., with B. Parish. Date of death and location of grave not ascertained. Enlisted March 1, 1778, serving one year in Company of Capt. Benjamin West, Col. John Topham's Reg't, Gen. Ezekiel Cornell's Brigade. In his application for pension Phineas Palmeter, a Revolutionary soldier of Busti, certified that he had been a comrade of Jonathan Dyer, enlisting at the same time and serving in the same company and regiment. Pension was granted.

FINDLEY, ALEXANDER—Born in Ireland about 1759. Died at Findley Lake, Chautauqua County, N. Y., Oct. 2, 1832. Grave in Cemetery, Findley Lake, town of Mina. Pennsylvania Historical Records say he came to America from Ireland, about 1763 or 1770, was the son of William Findley, who settled at Findleyville, Washington County, Pennsylvania. It is recorded that he was a Sergeant in Capt. Crawford's Company, Pennsylvania Militia, in the Revolutionary war. Penna. Archives, 6 series, vol. 2, pages 165, 171, 211, also Vol. 12, page 134, showing land purchase in Washington County. He enlisted and served also in the war of 1812 it is claimed as also did his son, William. Some of his descendants served in the Civil War of 1861-65, making three generations in the Findley family to prove their patriotism in battle. He was married to Nancy Mary Jane Carson, at Findleyville, Pa., in the year 1784, and their wedding trip was to Ireland, returning to America in 1787. In 1811 he obtained a concession of land from the Holland Land Company in the town of Mina, Chautauqua County, N. Y., and in 1816 moved to and made his home in that section, named after him, and now known as Findley Lake. His wife died June 27, 1857, aged 96 years, and her grave is beside husband. They had 11 children, 6 sons and 5 daughters, ten of whom arrived at mature age. Of the sons, Russel, Hugh, and Carson, settled in Mina.

HALE, JOSIAH—Born Aug. 21, 1756, at Enfield, Mass. Family records say that he came to Chautauqua County in the early part of the 19th century, settled on a farm in the town of Chautauqua where he died and is buried in Mayville Cemetery. He was a soldier in the American Revolution, serving as private in Capt. Noah Lankton's Company, Col. John Ashley's 1st Berkshire Co. Reg't. Enlisted July, 1777, and also in Sept., 1777. He was the son of William and Hannah Hale and a cousin of Nathan Hale, the famous Revolutionary patriot. In 1780, he married Abigail Joslin. Their children were: Nathan, 1st, Josiah, James, Nathan, 2nd, Esther, Jesse, Achsa, Abraham. The sons, Nathan and James, each settled on farms in the town of Chautauqua, near Mayville. James was a soldier in the war of 1812 and some years later left Chautauqua County and located in Michigan, where he died. He had two sons, James and Horace, also several daughters, who retained their residence in Chautauqua County. Horace Hale became a resident of Westfield at an early age and was one of the founders and a deacon in the First Baptist Church. His death occurred in 1895, leaving many descendants now living in Chautauqua County. John W. Hale, for many years a prominent and honored citizen of Jamestown, was the eldest son of Horace Hale. At the first call for troops, at the commencement of the Civil war, he enlisted in Company B., the first company to leave Chautauqua County in May, 1861.

HALL, JOHN—Born about 1757. Died Nov. 26, 1832, at Portland, Chautauqua County, N. Y. Grave supposed to be in Cemetery in town of Portland. Enlisted in 1776 at Ticonderoga, N. Y., in Capt. Down's Company, Col. Burrill's Reg't, serving one year. Enlisted in 1778 for nine months in 2nd New York Reg't, Col. Cortlandt, and was with the army at Valley Forge. Was taken prisoner at the battle of the Cedars in the Province of Canada during his first enlistment but soon after exchanged. Was present at the battle of Monmouth. Received his discharge Feb. 6, 1779, and according to family records served three months and later two months as a substitute for his father-in-law. He was united in marriage with Sarah Reynolds, daughter of Caleb Reynolds, June 7, 1781, at Pownel, Vt.

In 1837, Sarah Hall, widow of John Hall, was awarded a pension at which time she was 74 years of age. She is mentioned in the 1840 Pension List as residing in Westfield. In 1837 mention is made of a daughter, Maria Hall.

HOUGHTON, SILAS—Born Nov. 13, 1750, at Bolton, Mass. Died May 4, 1834, aged 84 years, 5 months and 20 days. Grave in Mayville Cemetery. Enlisted in May, 1775, while residing at Brattleborough, Vt., served as private in Capt. Benjamin Hasting's Company, Col. Asa Whitcomb's Massachusetts Reg't. Was in the Battle of Bunker Hill. Was later transferred to Capt. Jonathan Whitcomb's Company, Col. Asa Reed's New Hampshire Reg't, serving until March 20, 1776. Enlisted in April or May, 1776, served as private in Capt. Timothy Church's Company, Col. William's Reg't, New York troops, serving until November, 1776, and in June, 1777, he enlisted and served in same company and regiment until October, 1777. He was present at the battle of Bemus Heights. He was allowed a pension on his application executed in Sept., 1832, while a resident of Chautauqua County. A daughter, Rebecca Crippen, is referred to, a resident of Chautauqua.

HOUSE, JOHN, Deacon—Born in Morristown, N. J., June 23, 1760. Died in Westfield, N. Y., March 10, 1838. Grave in Union Cemetery, towns of Westfield and Portland. Enlisted at Morristown, N. J., in 1781, in Capt. Henry Kuster's Company, 3rd Battalion, Lancaster Co. Mil. In 1784 at Morristown married Joanna Prudden, daughter of Col. Prudden, and moved to Cortland County, N. Y., where their eight children were born. Later moved to Westfield, N. Y., and settled on land purchased of the Holland Land Company. The original deed is now in possession of his great grand-daughter, Cora E. House, who resides on a part of the original farm. The graves of Deacon John House and his wife, Joanna, are in Union Cemetery, Portland and Westfield, this being a part of his farm donated by him for a burying ground.

MADDEN, DAVID—Born 1763. Died March 16, 1843, aged 80 years. Grave in Cemetery, near Mina Corners, Chautauqua County, N. Y. His military record, as soldier in the Revolutionary war, from Mass. Soldiers and Sailors, page 128, says: "David Madden, Milford, private, Capt. Benj. Read's Company, Col. John Rand's Reg't, enlisted July 14, 1780, served three months, 7 days, incl. ten days, 200 miles travel home. Company stationed at West Point, raised in Worcester County to reinforce Continental army for three months, also served in Capt. Reuben Davis' Company, Col. Luke Drury's Reg't. Detached July 17, 1781, marched to join regiment, July 25, 1781, arrived at West Point, Aug. 1, 1781, was discharged Nov. 1, 1781, service 3 months, 22 days, including 9 days, 180 miles travel home. Residence Milford." His name appears in the Pension List of 1840, aged 77 years, as residing in the town of Mina with Ichabod Thayer.

McGREGOR, Captain DAVID—Born in the year 1744 at Mansfield, Mass. Died July 4, 1828. Grave in Mayville Cemetery Mayville, N. Y. He was the son of Rev. James McGregor, who was the pastor of the First Presbyterian Church in New England. He pursued a Collegiate course and was graduated from Dartmouth College in 1774. He entered service in the American army at Winter Hill, Mass., in June or July, 1775, as First

Lieutenant in Capt. Daniel Moore's Company, Col. John Stark's New Hampshire Regiment. He was commissioned Captain Aug. 4, 1777, and in Dec., 1778, was transferred to the 2nd New Hampshire Reg't, commanded by Lieut. Col. George Reid, and later served as Captain of a company designated at various times as Capt. David McGregor's 4th and 1st Company. His name last appears on the Company muster roll for April, 1783. He was allowed a pension on his application executed April 10, 1818, while residing at Romulus, Seneca County, N. Y. In 1820 he was living at Ripley, Chautauqua County, N. Y. He was married to Elizabeth Holland, who was born in 1764 and died in 1828. Their children were: Elizabeth, died in infancy; Stephen, born 1785, married Hulda Jones; David, born 1789, married Clarissa Munson; Mary, married William Van Dusen. Captain McGregor was a member of the first Masonic Lodge, organized in Londonderry, N. H.

MORSE, JOSIAH—Born 1763. Died May 21, 1839, aged 76 years. Grave in Findleys' Lake Cemetery, town of Mina. Enlisted April, 1781, at Worthington, Mass., as private in Capt. Stephen Clapp's Company of Artificers. Discharged Jan., 1782, at New Windsor, N. Y. Was at the battle of Yorktown. Granted pension in 1827 while residing at Mina, Chautauqua County, N. Y., at the age of 64 years. He was the son of Dr. Moses Morse of Worthington, Mass. Had seven brothers, all in the Revolutionary army, three of whom lost their lives. He was married at Cambridge, N. Y., May 30 or 31, 1791, to Emma Wetherbee, who was born at Wendell, Mass., Feb. 1, 1769. Their children were: Elisha, Nancy, Edwin, Nathan, Eliza, Clarissa, Charlotte, Emily. Widow was allowed pension in 1844 while a resident of Chautauqua County. She died at Chicago, Ill., June 17, 1855.

NICHOLS, JONATHAN—Born at Bolton, Mass., 1754. Died April 26, 1842, aged 88 years. Grave in Lower Ripley Cemetery with D. A. R. marker: "6 N. H. Mil. Rev. War." Enlisted in 1775, served four years, was wounded in the face at the battle of Bennington. Emigrated to western New York in 1813 with wife and nine children, which required a journey of two months, and on their arrival at Westfield at once commenced the erection of a log cabin in which they resided through the winter. His wife, Phebe, died Nov. 8, 1844, in the 77th year of her age. Their children were: Lorrel, Olney, Orvis, Achsah, Wiseman, Chloe, Jonathan, Lucinda.

PENFIELD, SAMUEL—Born Feb. 20, 1763, in Wallingford, Conn. Died Aug. 24, 1851, aged 88 years. Grave in Westfield Cemetery with D. A. R. marker: "Samuel Penfield, Meig's Conn. Mil. Rev. War." While living in Watertown, Litchfield County, Connecticut, he enlisted March 1, 1779, and served nine months as private in Capt. Jotham Curtis' Connecticut Company. He enlisted in May or June, 1780, and served six months as private in Capt. Edwards' Company, Col. Heman Swift's Connecticut Reg't; was in a skirmish below Totowa, near Fort Lee, where he was severly wounded in his left side. He enlisted March 1, 1781, and served nine months as private in Capt. Royce's Company, Colonel Meig's Connecticut Reg't and was in several skirmishes. He was allowed a pension on his application executed Oct. 12, 1832, while living in Westfield, Chautauqua County, N. Y., where he had removed from Chittenden County, Vermont. He is mentioned in the

Pension List of 1840 as residing in Westfield. His wife, Elizabeth, died Sept. 27, 1845, aged 88 years, and her grave is beside husband. They left two surviving children, Anna, the widow of Buel Howard, and Electa, the widow of John Howard.

RICE, Ensign PELETIAH—Born at Westbury, Mass., in 1754. Grave in Union Cemetery, towns of Westfield and Portland. Enlisted Jan., 1776, served 5 months under Capt. Samuel Wright, Col. Warner. Enlisted June, 1777, 1 month under Capt. Garino, Col. Warner. And in fall of 1778 served in Company of Capt. John Fassett and Col. Walbridge. Also served for a time during 1779 and 1781. His place of enlistment was Wallonsac, Rensselear County, N. Y. Government marker at his grave: "Ensign Rice, Vt. Mil." He is on Pension List of 1831, aged 79 years, and residing in Chautauqua County, N. Y.

RUMSEY, DAVID—Born in Redding, Conn., 1758. Died Jan. 2, 1849, in the 91st year of his age. Grave in Westfield Cemetery with D. A. R. marker: "6 Ct. Mil. Rev. War." Enlisted in Company Leavenworth, 1778, served ten months besides service in the armory at Springfield, Mass. Came to Westfield in 1831, settled on Rumsey farm, East Main Street, where he died in 1849. Hannah, his wife, died Feb. 14, 1841, aged 80 years. They had 10 children, among them Aaron and Calvin, who settled in Buffalo at an early date, and Stephen, who died in Westfield in 1873. He is mentioned in the Pension List of 1840.

SELDEN, BENJAMIN—Born in the year 1753. Died 1840. Grave in Sec. 1, lot 1, Sherman Cemetery, town of Sherman. Mrs. L.A. Loomis, who was a granddaughter, writing from Bear Lake, Pa., Sept. 23, 1913, says: "Benjamin Selden, buried in Sherman Cemetery, in 1840, nearly 88 years old, my grand-father, was a Revolutionary soldier."

SPENCER, ORANGE, Rev.—Born. July 30, 1764 or 1765, at Richmond, Mass. Died Jan. 10, 1843. Grave in Quincy Rural Cemetery, town of Ripley. He was the son of Jonathan Spencer, who was born 1744 and died 1821. While a resident of Warrensbrush, Tryon County, N. Y., he enlisted and served in the New York Militia as Musician and private, under Captains Lytle, Putnam, Yuman and Harrison, and Col. Willets. Was granted pension on application executed Sept. 21, 1832, while a resident of North East, Pa. He was united in marriage Dec. 4, 1787, to Sarah Bostwick, who was born Dec. 25, 1768, and died Jan. 24, 1845. Her grave is beside husband. Their children were: Philomelah, date of birth not ascertained, who was married in 1811 to John Fry; Ruth, and Orange B., born April, 179—, the former married Nehemiah Yale, in 1808, and Orange married Jemima Bostwick in 1812; Gains L., born 1794; Silvester, born 1796; Lena, born 1800, married Peter Loop, in 1817; Gilbert born 1804, married Evertine Gay, in 1825; Silas S., born 1809, married Jane Graham, in 1833. The known grandchildren are Alida and Lydia, daughters of Nehemiah and Ruth Yale.

STANDISH, AMOS—Born at Pembroke, Mass., 1750. Died at Portland, Chautauqua County, N. Y., Aug. 16, 1842. Grave supposed to be in Portland Cemetery. Enlisted at Livingston Manor, N. Y., 1775, serving in Capt. Herrick's Company, went to Ticonderoga, discharged Jan., 1776. Returned to Mass., enlisted same month at Roxbury under

Capt. Read, Col. John Bailey, following the British from Boston to New York. Suffered a broken leg at New York and at the end of his enlistment was discharged at Peekshill. Returned to Bridgewater, Mass., and enlisted in Company of Capt. Cole, Col. Bailey's Reg't. His final discharge was at North Kingston, R. I. He was united in marriage with Esther Kingsbury, at Dedham, Mass., Dec. 14, 1783. They resided in Thompson, Conn., for 20 years, and in 1835, he asked for a transfer of pension to New York state as he "is about to remove to, and is now on his way, to Chautauqua County, N. Y., where he intends to remain." His reason for asking the change is that his son-in-law resides there and he wishes to spend his remaining days with a beloved daughter. He and his wife remained at the home of their son-in-law, John Robbins, in Portland, until their death. Amos Standish claimed to be a direct descendant of the famous Miles Standish.

STETSON, OLIVER—Grave in Lower Ripley Cemetery with D. A. R. marker: "Bailey's Mass. Mil. Rev. War." Died Sept. 14, 1839. He came from Eastern New York and settled on land west of the town about 1827 and the family history credits him of serving in the greater portion of the Revolutionary war, and that he was also a soldier in the war of 1812, made a prisoner at the battle of Black Rock, taken to Montreal and a little later exchanged. During his residence in Ripley he became the Captain of a local military company. His wife, Jennet, died Dec. 23, 1825, in the 69th year of her age.

TENNANT, DANIEL—Born 1763. Died in 1850. Grave in Mayville Cemetery, on stone it says he was "Private, Col. Canfield's Reg't, Conn. Vols., 1781." Edison's history says: "Daniel Tennant emigrated from Scotland about 1748 and settled in Connecticut where his son, Daniel, was born about 1761, and when seventeen years of age entered the Revolutionary army; was at West Point at the time of the treason of Arnold, saw the American cannons spiked, and saw Major Andre after his capture. He married Miss Hale, of Irish birth. After the war he settled in Oneida County, N. Y., and in 1827 moved to Chautauqua County."

THAYER, JOSEPH—Born 1755. Died May 17, 1838. His funeral was held at Westfield, N. Y., and it is supposed he was buried in that town. He enlisted in the American army in 1775, served under Captain Curtis and Starr, Col. Hinman, Connecticut Militia. Re-enlisted in 1776, serving under Capt. Bostwick and Col. Webb. He was at the battles of Royalton, White Plains, and Trenton, and Bennington. Pension granted him in 1823. He was married May 8, 1776, at Kent, Litchfield County, Conn., to Abigail, daughter of Jonathan Sacket. Their children were Reuben and Anna, referred to at the time wife was granted pension in 1838. With his family he came to Chautauqua County in 1808 and settled on a tract of land where the County Poor House is now located in the town of Chautauqua. His wife, Abigail, after his death was granted a pension. She died at Mayville, April 18, 1845.

TURNER, WILLIAM—Born in 1753. Date of death not ascertained. Grave in Sherman Cemetery. Enlisted March 1st, 1777, and served 2 years and 4 months under Captains Edward Shipman and Tracey, Col. Chas. Webb and Col. Jedediah Huntington, Conn. Militia. Was twice wounded and once a prisoner.

Applied for pension in 1818 while residing at Killingsworth, Conn. He is mentioned in the Pension List of 1840 as residing in the town of Sherman, Chautauqua County, with his daughter Phebe M. Platt, wife of Richard Platt. In 1820, he referred to his wife, Phebe, 50 years of age, and his children: Dolly Ann and Phebe Maria.

WALDO, DAVID—Born Sept. 21, 1764, in Dover, Dutchess County, N. Y. Grave in Sherman Cemetery, town of Sherman. While living at Cambridge, Albany County, N. Y., he enlisted in 1779 and served 13 months as private under Captains Geo. Gilmore, John McKillig, Jos. Wells and Bradshaw, and Colonels Lewis VanWoert and Seth Sherwood in New York troops. His name appears on roll of 16th Reg't of Albany Co. Militia. He was granted a pension in 1833 while a resident of Mina, Chautauqua County, N. Y. He is mentioned in the Pension List of 1840 as living at Sherman. In 1852 he referred to his aged wife, name not given, and in 1854, at the age of 90 years, he was living in Sherman.

WELLS, ASA—Born at Hatfield, Mass., Dec. 15, 1763. Died at Chautauqua County, N. Y., in 1842. Grave in Volusia, Porter Cemetery, Westfield;. Served as private in Capt. Wells' Company, Col. Samuel Brewer's Reg't, Mass. Militia, for three months; served as private in Capt. Timothy Child's Company and Col. David Leonard's Reg't; served as private in Capt. Amasa Sheldon's Company, Col. Elisha Porter's Reg't; served as Fifer in Capt. Russel's 2nd Co. of Vol., 2nd Hampshire Co., for service against the insurgents of Northampton, 1782. Was the son of Samuel (the 5th) and Lucy Evans Wells, and was descended from Hugh Wells, John Wells, John Marsh, John Webster, William Hyde, and Stephen Post, whose names are on the Founder's Monument in Hartford, Conn., and also from Samuel Chapin, whose statue stands in the Art Institute at Springfield, Mass., so honored because he was instrumental in saving the lives of the inhabitants of that town during an Indian uprising. Asa Wells had two brothers who were also soldiers in the American army during the Revolution, David, a private, and Benjamin, an officer. In early life he married Elizabeth Smith and after her death he married, in 1815, Lydia Allis, daughter of John Allis, who was also a Revolutionary soldier. He emigrated to Westfield, N. Y., in 1830, driving through from New England in a covered wagon and settled at the "Gulf" Volusia. There was quite a large family of children, among them "Dollie" and David. Not any of his children are now living and most of the grand-children of the first wife have passed away; though there were ten grandchildren who were living in 1923, one of them, Mrs. Effie Wells Loucks, came from Minnesota to assist in locating his grave. Patterson Chapter D. A. R. placed a memorial stone at his grave in 1924. His wife, Lydia, is buried by his side.

WHEELER, SAMUEL—Was born in Westfield, Mass., in Jan., 1764. He died at Westfield, Chautauqua County, N. Y., May 23, 1847. He enlisted in the Continental army in 1780, serving in the 4th Mass. Reg't, receiving an honorable discharge at the end of the war. He was awarded pension and is mentioned in the Pension Lists of 1830 and 1840 as residing at Westfield, Chautauqua County, N. Y. He was buried on his farm on the Sherman road, near Westfield. All traces of the burial lot have since been removed. His older brother, Daniel, was an officer in Wayne's Regiment, and his younger brother, Moses, was in the same regiment with Samuel. In Feb., 1787, he married Ruby Dewey, who was born in 1767. She died in 1847. Their children were: Samuel, born June, 1788, who married Hannah King; Daniel, died at age of 6; Ruby, born 1793, married Eli Bisbee; Dewey, born 1796, married Hester Van Winkle; Clara, born 1798, married Levi Mills, and later L. Harrington; Laura, born 1802, married Thomas McClintock, she died Oct. 9, 1889; Daniel 2nd, born 1804, married Rebecca Hill, and died in 1880; Marion, born 1809, died March, 1861, became wife of Charles Hill. Many descendants of Samuel Wheeler and his wife, Ruby Dewey, are still living.

WINTERS, JUVENILE—Born March 18, 1762, at Pomfret, Windham County, Conn. Died Sept. 11, 1841, aged 79 years. Grave in Holdridge Corners' Cemetery, town of Mina, Chautauqua County, N. Y. Enlisted in June, 1778, and served thirty days as private in Captain Durkee's Connecticut Company. Enlisted in March, 1780, and served three months in Captain Johnson's Company, Col. Durkee's Connectict Reg't, serving nine months in all. Enlisted in Sept., 1781, served about twenty days in Captain William Osgood's Connecticut Company. Was granted pension in 1821 while residing at Ellisburgh, Jefferson Co., N. Y. Is mentioned in the pension list of 1840 as residing at Mina, Chautauqua County, N. Y. He was married in 1780, at Cherry Valley, N. Y., to Amelia Heath. She was allowed pension, after his death, while residing at Ripley, in 1849, and was at that time 80 years of age. They had ten children but only the following names are given: Samuel, Isaac, Clarissa, Sterling, Charles, Catherine, Joseph.

WRIGHT, REUBEN—Born in 1748 in New Britain, Conn. Died April 17, 1841, in the 93rd year of his age. Grave in Westfield Cemetery with D. A. R. marker: "Serg't Reuben Wright, 7th Ct. Mil. Rev. War." Enlisted in the 7th Connecticut Reg't and served several years, attained the rank of Sergeant. Came to Westfield in 1817 and bought land on the Wright Road where his son, James, afterward lived, and now owned by his great-grandson, A. S. Fitch. He was said to have been a remarkably strong man, over 6 feet in height and of powerful frame. His vitality was wonderful. He did a hard day's work the day before he died and passed away in his sleep, April 17, 1841. He is mentioned in the Pension List of 1840. Martha, his wife, died June 29, 1841, in the 86th year of her age, and is buried beside her husband. They left nine surviving children.

Location of Graves of Revolutionary Soldiers

ARKWRIGHT TOWNSHIP

Arkwright Cemetery
   Eliakim Thatcher
   William Wood
   James Olmstead

BUSTI TOWNSHIP

Frank Cemetery
   John Frank
   Lawrence Frank
   Reuben Landon

Hazeltine Cemetery
   John Jones

Elias Jenner Farm
   Levi Pier

Palmiter Cemetery
   John B. Smiley

Wellman Cemetery
   Barnabus Wellman

Wilcox Cemetery
   Stephen Wilcox

CARROLL TOWNSHIP

   Benjamin Covel
   John Owen (Grave in Warren, Pa.)

CHARLOTTE TOWNSHIP

   John Cleland
   Elias Carter
   Elijah Carter
   —— Carpenter
   Caleb Clark
   Robert W. Seaver

CHARLOTTE TOWNSHIP—*Continued*

Sinclairville Cemetery
   Jacob Gleason
   Nathaniel Johnson
   Samuel Sinclair

Pickett Cemetery
   Amos Atkins

CHAUTAUQUA TOWNSHIP

Mayville Cemetery
   Peter Barnhart
   Bethul Bond
   George Darrow
   Silas Houghton
   Capt. David McGregor
   Daniel Tennant, Sr.
   Jonathan Brigham
   Josiah Hale

Magnolia Cemetery
   Samuel Davis
   Adonijah Fenton
   Richard Whitney

Pleasantville Cemetery
   Elijah Look
   Levi Stedman
   Samuel Waterbury
   Nahum Parkhurst

Dewittville Cemetery
   Seeley Scofield
   Samuel Young

CLYMER TOWNSHIP

Clymer Cemetery
   John Campbell
   Gardiner Cleveland
   Daniel Williams
   Daniel Wing

LOCATION OF GRAVES

ELLERY TOWNSHIP

Bemus Point Cemetery
  Jonathan Babcock
  Lemuel Bacon
  Luther Barney
  William Bemus
  Benjamin Parker

Red-Bird Cemetery
  John Pickard
  John Coe

Lewis Cemetery
  Jacob Annis
  William Scofield
  Joseph Boyd

ELLICOTT TOWNSHIP

Fluvanna Cemetery
  Jacob Fenton
  Jeremiah Griffith
  Joseph Loucks
  William Martin
  John Rhodes
  William Smiley

Falconer Cemetery
  Paul Davis

JAMESTOWN CITY

Lake View Cemetery
  Andrew Crawford
  Joseph Dix
  Cyrus Fish
  Daniel Hazeltine
  Isaac Staples
  Eliphalet Steward

Old Cemetery
  Thomas Mathews
  Benjamin DeLamater
  William Washburn

ELLINGTON TOWNSHIP

Ellington Cemetery
  Abijah Hitchcock

Clear Creek Cemetery
  Stephen Mather

FRENCH CREEK TOWNSHIP
  William Adams

GERRY TOWNSHIP

Gerry Hill Cemetery
  Benjamin Mathews

HANOVER TOWNSHIP

Glenwood Cemetery, Silver Creek
  John Darling
  John Johnson

Doty Cemetery
  Jesse Clothier
  Shibnah Spink

Smith's Mills Cemetery
  Asa Gage

Rathbun Cemetery
  Solomon Rathbun

Nashville Cemetery
  Silas Nash
  Thomas Frink
  Enos Schofield

Ball Town Cemetery
  William Kirkland

Hanover Center Cemetery
  Amos Ingraham
  Thomas Nevins

Pioneer Cemetery, Forestville
  John Ferry
  Susannah, wife of John Ferry
  Robert Love
  Reuben Barnes
  Isaac Van Camp
  Christopher McManus

LOCATION OF GRAVES

HARMONY TOWNSHIP

Ashville Cemetery
 Samuel Benedict
 David Hollister
 John Stow

Blockville Cemetery
 Simon Loomis
 Jonas Randall

Panama Cemetery
 Isaac Osborn

Niobe Cemetery
 Nathaniel Mather

Stowe, Connolly Farm
 William Matteson

Town Line Cemetery
 Phineas Chamberlain

KIANTONE TOWNSHIP

Kiantone Cemetery
 Ebenezer Cheney
 Asa Moore

Stillwater Cemetery
 Jasper Marsh
 Aaron Martin
 Capt. William Stearns

MINA TOWNSHIP

Mina Cemetery
 David Madden

Holdridge Corners Cemetery, Mina
 Juvenile Winters

Findley Lake Cemetery
 Alexander Findley
 Josiah Morse

POLAND TOWNSHIP

Allen Cemetery
 Phineas Allen
 Nathaniel Fenton
 Elias Tracey
 Joshua Woodward

Levant Cemetery
 Seth Baker

Dry Brook Cemetery
 Jonathan Bill
 John Tucker

Riverside Cemetery
 Cyrus Hamlin
 John Woodward

POMFRET TOWNSHIP

In or near Fredonia
 Thomas Abel
 Hezekiah Barker
 John Brigham
 Seth Cole
 Simon Crosby
 Roswell Fitch
 Veniah Fox
 Luther Gates
 Nathaniel Hempstead
 William Hood
 King Moore
 Jonathan Phelps
 Jeremiah Rood
 Joseph Rood
 Elijah Risley
 William Seymour
 Reuben Thompson
 Elisha Webster
 William Lamont

Laona Cemetery
 Augustus Burnham
 Israel Smith

LOCATION OF GRAVES

PORTLAND TOWNSHIP
Daniel Barnes
John Coney
Samuel Munson
Capt. James Dunn
Joseph Gugle
James Goldsmith
Zimri Hill
Peter Kane
Willoughby Lowell
John Light
Jeremiah Potter
Joseph Phelps Peters
Samuel Parker
Samuel Shattuck
Samuel Tucker
Reuben Taylor
John Hall
Amos Standish

RIPLEY TOWNSHIP
Ripley Cemetery
Levi Adams
Downs Cemetery
Benjamin Bennet
East Ripley Cemetery
Arthur Bell
Robert Dickson
Jonathan Nichols
Oliver Stetson
Quincy Rural Cemetery
Orange Spencer

SHERMAN TOWNSHIP
William Turner
Benjamin Seldens
David Waldo

STOCKTON TOWNSHIP
Stockton Cemetery
Abraham Batcheler
Daniel Deming
Ebenezer Smith
Asa Turner
Thomas Curtice

SHERIDAN TOWNSHIP
Sheridan Cemetery
Rev. John Spencer
Ephriam Herrick
Samuel Cranston
Moses Allen
Nathan Thompson
Stephen Bush
James White
Otis Ensign

VILLENOVA TOWNSHIP
Villenova Cemetery
Mathias Ball
John Kent
Solomon Naughton
Daniel Osborn
Thomas Phillips
Reuben Spencer
Hamlet Cemetery
Lieut. Elias Clark
Nathaniel Warner

WESTFIELD TOWNSHIP
Westfield Cemetery
Corp. Lent Bradley
Nathaniel Bird
David Burnham
Fiske Durand
Jonathan Dyer
William Chase
Samuel Penfield
David Rumsey
Joseph Thayer
Samuel Wheeler
Reuben Wright
Union Cemetery, Westfield and West Portland
Samuel Anderson
William Couch
David House
John House
Peletiah Rice
Velutia Cemetery
Asa Wells

The graves of quite a number of Revolutionary soldiers who lived and died in Chautauqua County have not been located.

Appendix

It is certain that there are a number of names of Revolutionary Soldiers who were at one time residents of Chautauqua County that are not included in the lists prepared by the D. A. R. Chapters in the preceding pages. It is because so little of authentic facts have at the present time been obtained of the personal or military history, although it is quite likely that later research may supply much that will prove valuable and interesting.

The following list of names of Revolutionary Soldiers are included in the Pension Lists of 1818 and 1830, on file at the Bureau of Pensions, Washington, D. C., and who at one time were residents of Chautauqua County, N. Y., while receiving their pensions:

Name	Rank	State	Pension Date	Age
Andrews, Amos	Private	Mass.	1828	—
Barlow, Abner	Private	N. H.	1818	75
Bidwell, Phineas	Private	Conn.	1831	71
Burch, Thomas	Private	N. Y.	1831	71
Burdick, Gideon	Private	N. Y.	1831	71
Clark, Roger	Private	Conn.	1818	73
Cook, Joel	Private	Conn.	1818	74
Colfax, Samuel	Private	Vt.	1831	79
Davis, Joseph	Private	Mass.	1831	71
Denny, Charles	Private	Mass.	1831	74
Doty, Ellis	Private	Mass.	1818	71
Fitch, Rufus	Sergeant	Conn.	1818	80
Fairchild, John	Private	N. Y.	1831	86
Green, Timothy	Private	N. Y.	1824	68
Hosier, John	Private	N. Y.	1818	66
Hunt, Elvin	Private	N. Y.	1831	74
Hill, Benoni	Private	N. H.	1818	72
Ives, Amasa	Private	Mass.	1831	86
Jenkins, Joseph	Private	Mass.	1831	80
Lesner, John	Ensign	Mass.	1818	82
Loomis, Israel	Private	Mass.	1818	64
Matoon, Abel	Private	Mass.	1819	82
Merrill, Noah	Private	Conn.	1818	62
Morse, Artimus	Private	Mass.	1817	—
Mumford, Henry	Private	Mass.	1831	70
Pitcher, Abner	Private	Conn.	1818	78
Plummer, Simeon	Private	N. Y.	1818	79
Sprague, William	Private	R. I.	1831	69
Smith, Elisha	Private	Vt.	1831	74
Skinner, Jesse	Private	N. Y.	1831	83

APPENDIX

Name	Rank	State	Pension Date	Age
Tyler, Jonathan	Private	N. H.	1824	58
Truesdell, Hiel	Private	N. Y.	1831	70
Tifft, Rufus	Private	N. Y.	1831	79
Wilson, Alexander	Private	Mass.	1818	72
Willard, Ephriam	Private	Mass.	1818	74
Webster, William	Private	Conn.	1831	75
Williams, John	Sergeant	Conn.	1831	89
Whitney, John	Private	Mass.	1818	74

The name of JOEL ANDREWS appears on the pension list of 1818 as residing in Chautauqua County, name of place not stated. The New Hampshire Historical Society gives his record as follows: "Born in 1753. Died in Chautauqua County, June 26, 1825. Married Anna ——, June 1, 1786. She was born 1760 and died 1841. The Massachusetts record shows that he was of Charlestown, N. H. Enlisted in 1775 under Capt. Seth Murray, Col. Woodbridge; re-enlisted under Capt. Gilman, Col. Nixon, Sept. to Nov., 1776. N. H. rolls show him as on Lt.-Col. Hammond's return, Swanzey, Feb. 14, 1778, as lately enlisted, also in Capt. Abel Walker's Company, Col. Benj. Bellows' Reg't.

HASADIAH STEBBINS, born in 1754, served as private in Capt. Joseph Thompson's Company, Col. Daniel's Reg't, Mass. Line. He was born at Monson, Mass., and died in Chautauqua County, N. Y., in the year 1824. He married Betsey Sessions Babcock, in 1777. The above is the record in Lin. Vol. 74, p. 102.

There is a grave in Charlotte Cemetery, town of Charlotte, of a man who is said to have been a Revolutionary soldier, of the name of CARPENTER. But no authentic personal or military record of him has been obtained.

NAHUM PARKHURST, born about 1767. Died Aug. 28, 1833. Grave in Pleasantville Cemetery, town of Chautauqua. Not any record of his services as a soldier of the Revolution has been obtained except from the headstone at his grave, which is inscribed: "With Wayne in battle, side by side, unharmed our hero fought." His wife, Abigail, died May 6, 1850, aged 78 years, 1 month and 6 days. Her grave is beside husband. He is not mentioned in any of the Chautauqua County Census Pension Lists. He settled in the town of Chautauqua in the year 1817.

JONAS RANDALL is the name of a man who may have been a soldier of the American Revolution, whose grave, without headstone, is in Blockville Cemetery, town of Harmony. He was born in 1754 and died in 1838. No record of his personal or military history has been found.

JOHN TUCKER, said to have been a Revolutionary soldier, but no record of his services has been obtained. Born about 1765, died January 27, 1852. Grave in Dry Brook Cemetery, town of Poland. No mention of him in Pension Lists.

APPENDIX

JOHN FRANK, who was one of the early settlers of the town of Busti, born about 1743, in Germany, died Nov. 5, 1833, grave in Hatch Cemetery, Busti, may have been a soldier in the Revolution, although no record of his services has been obtained. He is not mentioned in the Pension Lists. His wife, Eve, according to family records, was as a child captured by Indians, taken to Canada, where she remained 3 years.

The Centennial History of Chautauqua County, 1904, says HENRY ELLIOTT, at one time a resident of the town of Chautauqua, was a soldier of the Revolution, was badly wounded in the campaign against Burgoyne, afterwards served on the ship Putnam, which in its cruise off the coast of England, captured nine prizes. No further record obtained.

Although not a resident of Chautauqua County, GIDEON NORTHRUP, a Revolutionary soldier, spent the latter part of his life at Pine Grove, Warren County, Pa., just across the line from Chautauqua County, where he was a familiar figure in his day, and where he left many descendants. He served in Col. Webb's Reg't, Conn. Militia, during a part of the war. Was granted a pension in 1832. Grave in State Road Cemetery, Farmington, Pa.

The Mayville Sentinel, in its issue of July 6, 1848, says: "ELKANAH PHILLIPS, a soldier of the Revolution, and a native of Grafton, N. H., died recently in the town of Carroll."

JEREMIAH WRIGHT, born in 1745, died in 1830, is the name of a man whose grave is located in the Forestville Cemetery, town of Hanover. No record of his personal history has been found, although it is the early impression of many that he was a Revolutionary soldier.

MARY STACY EATON, widow of Benjamin Eaton, a Revolutionary soldier, is mentioned in the Pension List of 1840, aged 87 and residing with David Eaton in the town of Portland, Chautauqua County, N. Y. Husband was at the battle of Lexington and later served in the Mass. Reg't of Col. Thomas Nixon. They were married the day after the battle of Lexington. Husband died in the year 1800 and in 1806 she came to Chautauqua County with her son. She died in Portland, Oct. 14, 1848, aged 95 years, 6 months and 1 day.

COMFORT HARRINGTON, widow of William Harrington, is mentioned in the Pension List of 1840, aged 86, and residing in the town of Hanover, Chautauqua County, N. Y., with Andrew Irish, son-in-law. Her husband, William Harrington, enlisted in 1775, serving in Capt. Grave's Company, Mass. troops, and was in the battle of Bennington and White Plains. He died at Luzerne, N. Y., in 1820. She applied for and was granted pension in 1838. They had five children.

APPENDIX

ELIZABETH CRANE, widow of Curtis Crane, Revolutionary soldier, is mentioned in the Pension List of 1840, aged 86, and residing with Elizabeth Howes, in the town of Pomfret, Chautauqua County, N. Y. Curtis Crane and Elizabeth were married at Weathersfield, Conn., in 1774. He enlisted in 1778, serving in Capt. Walker's Company, Col. Webb's Reg't, Conn. troops, attaining the rank of Corporal. He died Oct. 14, 1824, at Eaton, Madison County, N. Y.

LUCY HEACOX INGHAM, widow of Isaac Ingham, is mentioned in the Pension List of 1840 as residing in the town of Pomfret, Chautauqua County, at the age of 83 years. Her husband, Isaac Ingham, died at Sherburne, N. Y., in 1828. He served three years in Revolutionary war in Company of Capt. Buckley, Col. Webb, and in Company of Capt. Mills, Col. Willis' Reg't, Conn. troops. Was in the battle of Bunker Hill. In 1838 widow was living with her son, Isaac Ingham, Jr., in the town of Arkwright, Chautauqua County, N. Y.

HANNAH EVENS, widow of Joseph Evens, is mentioned in the 1840 Pension List, aged 78, as residing in the town of Arkwright, Chautauqua County, N. Y. Her husband served in Capt. Janson's Company, Col. Van Schaick's Reg't, N. Y. troops, during a portion of the Revolutionary war. He died in 1831 while on a visit to his son-in-law, Stephen Hill, at Arkwright. Hannah died Jan. 28, 1845.

SUSANNA SWIFT, widow of Samuel Swift, Revolutionary soldier, is mentioned in the Pension List of 1840, aged 70 years, and residing with her son, Lyman Swift, in the town of Sheridan, Chautauqua County, N. Y. He enlisted in 1778 and again in 1779, serving in Reg't of Col. Topins and in Col. Allen's Reg't, as private, Vt. troops. He died in 1821 at Elba, Genesee Co., N. Y., where they were at that time residing. She also resided for a time with her son, Clark C. Swift, in the town of Hanover.

SARAH MATTESON, widow of David Matteson, is mentioned in the Pension List of 1840, aged 85 years, and residing with D. J. Matteson at Fredonia, Chautauqua County, N. Y. Husband was Serg't in Vermont Militia under Captains Huntington and Galusha, and participated in the battles of Ticonderoga and Bennington. His death occurred in 1818 at Shaftsbury, Vt.

ASA SEYMOUR is said to have been a Revolutionary soldier, residing at Fredonia at an early date, as shown by the following notice printed in the Chautauqua Gazette, published at Fredonia, in the issue of May 18, 1818: "Died in this village last evening of a lingering illness, Mr. Asa Seymour in the 59th year of his age. A veteran soldier, he served his country faithfully for 6 years in the Revolutionary war, and had just made the affidavit necessary for obtaining his pension. A devout Christian, he has gone to receive an inheritance in Heaven. The funeral to be attended to-morrow at 1 o'clock P. M."

Index of Names of Soldiers

	Page		Page
Abel, Thomas	13	Burnham, Daniel	54
Adams, Levi	53	Bush, Stephen	43
Adams, William	23		
Allen, Moses	43	Campbell, John	25
Allen, Phineas	9	Carpenter, ——	67
Anderson, Samuel	53	Carter, Elias	14
Andrews, Amos	71	Carter, Elijah	14
Andrews, Joel	72	Chamberlain, Phineas	26
Annis, Jacob	23	Chase, William	57
Atkins, Amos	13	Cheney, Ebenezer	26
		Clark, Caleb	14
Babcock, Jonathan	23	Clark, Elias	43
Bacon, Lemuel	24	Clark, Roger	71
Baker, Seth	9	Cleland, John	14
Barnes, Calvin	53	Cleveland, Gardiner	27
Barnes, Daniel	13	Clothier, Jesse	44
Barnes, Reuben	43	Coe, John	27
Ball, Mathias	43	Colfax, Samuel	71
Barlow, Abner	71	Cook, Joel	71
Barker, Hezekiah	13	Cole, Seth	14
Barney, Luther	24	Comstock, Martin L.	27
Barnhart, Peter	54	Coney, John	15
Batcheller, Abraham	13	Cooley, Abner	44
Beebe, Amon	25	Cowing, John	28
Bell, Arthur	54	Couch, William	57
Bemus, William	25	Covel, Benjamin	28
Benedict, Samuel	25	Crane, Elizabeth	74
Bennett, Benjamin	54	Cranston, Samuel	44
Benson, Joel	54	Crawford, Andrew	28
Bidwell, Phineas	71	Crosby, Simon	15
Bill, Jonathan	9	Curtice, Thomas	15
Bird, Nathaniel	55		
Bond, Bethuel	55	Darling, John	44
Bovee, Nicholas	14	Darrow, George	57
Boyd, Joseph	25	Davis, Joseph	71
Bradley, Lent	56	Davis, Paul	9
Brigham, Jonathan	56	Davis, Samuel	28
Brigham, John	14	Delemater, Benjamin	28
Burch, Thomas	71	Deming, Daniel	15
Burdick, Gideon	71	Denny, Charles	71
Burnham, Augustus	14	Dickson, Robert	57

INDEX

Name	Page	Name	Page
Dix, Joseph	29	Herrick, Ephriam	46
Doty, Ellis	71	Hill, Benoni	71
Durand, Fisk	58	Hill, Zimri	16
Dunn, James	15	Hitchcock, Abijah	10
Dustin, Moses	58	Holmes, Orsamus	45
Dyer, Jonathan	58	Hollister, David	31
		Hood, William	17
Eaton, Mary Stacy	73	Hosier, John	71
Elliott, Henry	73	Houghton, Silas	60
Ely, William	29	House, John	60
Ensign, Otis	44	Hunt, Elvin	71
Evens, Hannah	44		
		Ives, Amasa	71
Fairchild, John	71	Ives, Enos	31
Fenton, Adonijah	29	Ingraham, Amos	46
Fenton, Jacob	29	Ingraham, William	46
Fenton, Nathaniel	10	Ingham, Lucy Heacock	74
Ferry, John	44		
Ferry, Susannah	45	Jenkins, Joseph	71
Findley, Alexander	58	Jones, John	31
Fish, Cyrus	30	Johnson, John	47
Fitch, Roswell	15	Johnson, Nathaniel	17
Fitch, Rufus	71		
Fox, Veniah	16	Kane, Peter	17
Frank, John	73	Kent, John	47
Frank, Lawrence	30	Kirkland, William	47
Frink, Thomas	45		
		Lamont, William	17
Gage, Asa	45	Landon, Reuben	32
Gates, Luther	16	Lesner, John	71
Gleason, Jacob	16	Light, John	17
Goldsmith, James	16	Look, Elijah	32
Gregory, Esbon	45	Loomis, Israel	71
Green, Timothy	71	Loomis, Simon	32
Griffith, Jeremiah	30	Lowell, Willoughby	18
Gugle, Joseph	16	Loucks, Joseph	32
		Love, Robert	47
Hale, Josiah	59		
Hall, John	59	Madden, David	60
Hamlin, Cyrenus	10	Maples, Josiah	32
Hamlin, Zacchias	46	Marsh, Jasper	33
Harrington, Comfort	73	Marsh, Silas	18
Hatch, Nathan	45	Martin, Aaron	33
Hazeltine, Daniel	31	Martin, William	33
Hemstead, Nathaniel	16	Mather, Joseph	47

INDEX

Name	Page
Mather, Nathaniel	33
Mather, Stephen	10
Mathews, Benjamin	11
Mathews, Thomas	34
Matteson, William	34
Matteson, Sarah	74
Matoon, Abel	71
McGregor, Capt. David	60
McManus, Christopher	47
Merrill, Noah	71
Moore, Asa	34
Moore, King	18
Morse, Artimus	71
Morse, Josiah	61
Mumford, Henry	71
Munson, Samuel	18
Nash, Silas	48
Naughton, Solomon	48
Nevins, Thomas	48
Nichols, Jonathan	61
Northrup, Gideon	73
Olmstead, James	48
Osborne, Daniel	48
Osborne, Isaac	35
Owen, John	35
Parker, Benjamin	35
Parker, Samuel	18
Palmiter, Phineas	35
Parkhurst, Nahum	72
Penfield, Samuel	61
Peters, Joseph Phelps	18
Phelps, Cornelius	48
Phelps, Jonathan	19
Phillips, Thomas	49
Phillips, Elkanah	73
Pickard, John	36
Pier, Levi	36
Pitcher, Abner	71
Plummer, Simeon	71
Potter, Jeremiah	19
Pratt, Stephen	49
Randall, Jonas	72
Rathbun, Solomon	49
Reynolds, Joel	11
Rhodes, John	36
Rice, Pelatiah	62
Risley, Elijah	19
Rood, Jeremiah	19
Rood, Joseph	19
Rumsey, David	62
Scofield, Enos	49
Scofield, Seely	36
Scofield, William	37
Seaver, Robert W.	20
Seldens, Benjamin	62
Seymour, Asa	74
Seymour, William	20
Shattuck, Samuel	20
Sinclair, Samuel	20
Skinner, Jesse	71
Smith, Ebenezer	21
Smith, Elisha	71
Smith, Israel	21
Smiley, John B.	37
Smiley, William	37
Spencer, Orange	62
Spencer, John	49
Spencer, Reuben	49
Spink, Shibnah	50
Sprague, William	71
Standish, Amos	62
Staples, Isaac	37
Stearns, Capt. William	38
Stetson, Oliver	63
Stedman, Levi	38
Steward, Eliphalet	38
Stebbins, Hasadiah	72
Stone, Isaac	21
Stow, John	38
Swift, Susannah	74
Taylor, Reuben	21
Tennant, Daniel	63
Thatcher, Eliakim	50

INDEX

	Page		Page
Thayer, Joseph	63	Wells, Asa	64
Thompson, Nathan	50	Wheeler, Samuel	64
Thompson, Reuben	21	Whitney, John	72
Tifft, Rufus	72	Whitney, Richard	40
Tracey, Elias	11	White, James	51
Truesdell, Hiel	72	Wiard, Darius	22
Tucker, John	72	Wilcox, Stephen	40
Tucker, Samuel	22	Williams, Daniel	40
Turner, Asa	22	Williams, John	72
Turner, William	63	Wilson, Alexander	72
Tylar, Jonathan	72	Willard, Ephriam	72
		Wing, Daniel	40
Van Camp, Isaac	50	Winters, Juvenile	65
		Wood, Charles	41
Waldo, David	64	Wood, Nathan	22
Walker, Lewis	22	Wood, William	51
Warner, Nathaniel	50	Woodward, John	11
Washburn, William	39	Woodward, Joshua	11
Waterbury, Samuel	39	Wright, Jeremiah	73
Webster, William	72	Wright, Reuben	65
Webster, Elisha	22		
Wellman, Barnabus	39	Young, Samuel	41
Wellman, John	39		

www.ingramcontent.com/pod-product-compliance
Lightning Source LLC
LaVergne TN
LVHW051156080426
835508LV00021B/2656